THE COMPLETE HIGH-PROTEIN LOW-CARB COOKBOOK FOR BEGINNERS

Delicious, Nutritious Recipes and a 4-Week Balanced Meal Plan for Enhancing Your Daily Energy | Full Color Edition

Renee R. Legere

Manufactured in the United States of America
Interior and Cover Designer: Danielle Rees
Art Producer: Brooke White
Editor: Aaliyah Lyons
Production Editor: Sienna Adams
Production Manager: Sarah Johnson
Photography: Michael Smith

TABLE OF CONTENTS

TABLE OF CONTENTS

TABLE OF CONTENTS

INTRODUCTION

Cooking has always been a cherished part of my life, but it wasn't until I faced a personal health challenge that I truly discovered the transformative power of food. A few years ago, I was diagnosed with high blood sugar and struggled with my weight. The doctor's words were a wake-up call: I needed to make significant changes to my diet.

At first, the idea of a high-protein, low-carb diet seemed overwhelming. I was used to comfort foods rich in carbs and sugars. But necessity drove me to explore new recipes and ingredients. I immersed myself in the world of high-protein, low-carb cooking, determined to find dishes that were both nutritious and enjoyable.

My kitchen became a laboratory of sorts. I experimented with different ingredients, learning to substitute traditional carb-heavy items with healthier alternatives. I remember the first time I successfully created a high-protein, low-carb version of my favorite pasta dish. It was a game-changer, both for my taste buds and my

health. I felt more energetic, my blood sugar levels stabilized, and the weight began to come off.

Sharing these recipes and my journey with others became a passion. I wanted to show that a high-protein, low-carb lifestyle didn't have to be bland or restrictive. Each recipe in this cookbook represents not just a meal but a piece of my transformation and a step toward a healthier life.

I hope this book inspires you to embrace the benefits of a high-protein, low-carb diet. It's not just about food; it's about reclaiming your health and feeling your best every day.

DEDICATION

To Dr. John, I wanted to extend my heartfelt thanks for your invaluable help and guidance during my journey towards healthier living. Your expertise and support have been instrumental in clarifying my path and making the transition to a high-protein, low-carb lifestyle a successful one. Your insights have not only improved my understanding of nutrition but have also empowered me to make lasting changes. I truly appreciate the time and effort you've invested in helping me. Your encouragement has been a key factor in achieving my health goals. Thank you for being such a crucial part of my journey.

CHAPTER 1: EMBRACING A HIGH-PROTEIN, LOW-CARB LIFESTYLE

WHY CHOOSE A HIGH-PROTEIN, LOW-CARB DIET?

Choosing a high-protein, low-carb diet can be a game-changer for your health and wellness. Let's break down why this diet might be right for you, starting with a closer look at proteins and carbohydrates, and how they impact your body.

UNDERSTANDING PROTEIN AND CARBOHYDRATES

Protein and carbohydrates are two of the three macronutrients that your body needs to function properly. Each plays a unique role in your overall health.

Protein is made up of amino acids, which are the building blocks for your muscles, skin, enzymes, and hormones. It's essential for repair and growth, which is why it's so important if you're active or looking to build muscle. When you eat protein, your body breaks it down into these amino acids and uses them to rebuild and maintain tissues. Good sources of protein include chicken, fish, eggs, beans, and tofu.

Carbohydrates, on the other hand, are your body's main source of energy. They get broken down into glucose, which your cells use for fuel. Carbs are found in foods like bread, pasta, fruits, and vegetables. However, not all carbs are created equal. Refined carbs and sugars can lead to weight gain and other health issues, while complex carbs like whole grains and vegetables provide lasting energy and essential nutrients.

HOW PROTEIN SUPPORTS YOUR BODY

So, why should you focus on protein in your diet? Protein has several benefits that can make a big difference in your health:

- **Muscle Repair and Growth:** After a workout, your muscles need protein to repair and grow stronger. If you're exercising regularly, consuming enough protein can help you recover faster and build muscle more effectively.

- **Satiety and Weight Management:** Protein is great for feeling full. It takes longer to digest compared to carbohydrates, which means you'll feel satisfied longer and are less likely to snack mindlessly. This can help with weight management by reducing overall calorie intake.

- **Metabolic Boost:** Digesting protein requires more energy than digesting carbs or fats. This means your body burns more calories processing protein, which can give your metabolism a boost.

THE ROLE OF LOW-CARB EATING IN WEIGHT MANAGEMENT

Switching to a low-carb diet can also have a significant impact on weight management:

STABILIZING BLOOD SUGAR LEVELS

Low-carb diets can help stabilize blood sugar levels by reducing the amount of glucose entering your bloodstream. This can be particularly beneficial for people with insulin resistance or type 2 diabetes. With fewer carbs, your blood sugar doesn't spike and crash as much, which means fewer cravings and more stable energy levels.

BURNING FAT FOR ENERGY

When you cut down on carbs, your body has to find an alternative source of energy. It starts to break down stored fat into ketones, which can be used as fuel.

This process, known as ketosis, helps your body become more efficient at burning fat.

REDUCING INSULIN LEVELS

High-carb diets can cause your body to produce more insulin, a hormone that promotes fat storage. By reducing carbs, you lower insulin levels, which can help with fat loss and improve overall metabolic health.

GETTING STARTED WITH YOUR NEW LIFESTYLE

Embarking on a high-protein, low-carb lifestyle is an exciting step towards better health and fitness. To make your transition smooth and successful, it's important to set yourself up with the right tools, ingredients, and strategies. Here's a practical guide to help you get started.

ESSENTIAL KITCHEN TOOLS AND INGREDIENTS

First things first: setting up your kitchen for success. You don't need a ton of fancy gadgets, but having a few key tools and ingredients on hand can make your new eating plan much easier to stick with.

KITCHEN TOOLS:

SHARP KNIVES

A good set of sharp knives makes meal prep a breeze. You'll need them for chopping vegetables, slicing meats, and more. Invest in a chef's knife, a paring knife, and a serrated knife for versatility.

CUTTING BOARD

A sturdy cutting board provides a safe and clean surface for preparing your food. Consider getting one for meats and one for fruits and vegetables to avoid cross-contamination.

NON-STICK COOKWARE

Non-stick pans are perfect for cooking up protein-rich foods like eggs and fish without needing extra oil. A good skillet and a baking sheet are essentials.

MEASURING CUPS AND SPOONS

Accurate measurements can be crucial when you're adjusting your diet. They help ensure you're sticking to portion sizes and balancing your macros correctly.

INGREDIENTS:

- **Lean Proteins:** Stock up on chicken breast, turkey, lean cuts of beef, fish, and eggs. These are your main sources of protein and will form the backbone of your meals.

- **Low-Carb Vegetables:** Vegetables like spinach, kale, broccoli, cauliflower, and bell peppers are low in carbs and high in nutrients. They'll add flavor, crunch, and variety to your dishes.

- **Healthy Fats:** Incorporate sources of healthy fats such as avocados, nuts, seeds, and olive oil. These will help keep you full and add flavor to your meals.

- **Herbs and Spices:** A range of herbs and spices can transform your meals from bland to delicious. Garlic, turmeric, cumin, and fresh herbs like cilantro or basil are great choices.

TIPS FOR TRANSITIONING SMOOTHLY

Transitioning to a high-protein, low-carb lifestyle can be a big change, but it doesn't have to be overwhelming. Here are some tips to make the process smoother:

PLAN YOUR MEALS

Start by planning your meals for the week. This helps you stay organized and prevents you from reaching for convenience foods that don't fit your new diet. Make a meal plan and create a shopping list based on the recipes you've chosen.

PREP AHEAD

Meal prep can save you time and keep you on track. Cook in bulk and store meals in the fridge or freezer. This way, you always have a healthy option ready to go, even on busy days.

STAY HYDRATED

Drinking enough water is essential, especially when adjusting to a lower-carb diet. Sometimes your body retains water when you first cut carbs, so staying hydrated helps flush out excess water and keeps things running smoothly.

LISTEN TO YOUR BODY

As you transition, pay attention to how your body responds. You might experience some changes, like increased energy or even the "keto flu" (if you're going extremely low-carb).

SETTING REALISTIC GOALS AND

EXPECTATIONS

Setting realistic goals and expectations is crucial for long-term success. Here's how to approach it:

- **Start Small:** Set achievable goals that you can build on over time. For instance, aim to incorporate more protein-rich meals into your week before tackling more complex dietary changes.

- **Track Your Progress:** Keep a food journal or use an app to track what you eat and how you feel. This helps you stay accountable and spot any patterns or areas where you might need to adjust.

- **Be Patient:** Dietary changes can take time to show results. Focus on the positive changes you're making and be patient with yourself. Progress might be slow at first, but consistency is key.

- **Celebrate Milestones:** Celebrate your successes, whether it's sticking to your meal plan for a week or hitting a personal health goal. Recognizing and rewarding yourself can keep you motivated.

NAVIGATING YOUR MEAL PLAN

To make the most of this lifestyle, it's essential to understand how to structure your daily meals and balance protein and carbohydrates effectively. Here's a practical guide to help you navigate your meal plan with ease.

STRUCTURING YOUR DAILY MEALS

A well-structured meal plan helps you stay on track and ensures you're meeting your nutritional needs. Here's a simple approach to organizing your daily meals:

- **Start with Breakfast:** Begin your day with a protein-rich breakfast to kickstart your metabolism and keep you full until your next meal. Consider options like scrambled eggs with spinach, Greek yogurt with berries, or a protein smoothie. Incorporate healthy fats like avocado or nuts to keep you satisfied.

- **Plan Your Lunch:** For lunch, aim for a balanced plate with a serving of lean protein, non-starchy vegetables, and a small portion of healthy fats. Think grilled chicken with a side of roasted Brussels sprouts and a drizzle of olive oil. If you're on the go, a salad with tuna or chicken and a few slices of avocado works well too.

- **Prepare a Filling Dinner:** Dinner should be hearty but still aligned with your high-protein, low-carb goals. Opt for dishes like baked salmon with a side of steamed broccoli or a beef stir-fry with bell peppers. The key is to focus on high-quality protein and low-carb vegetables.

- **Snacks and Hydration:** If you get hungry between meals, choose snacks that fit your plan, such as a handful of almonds, a piece of cheese, or veggie sticks with hummus. Don't forget to drink plenty of water throughout the day. Staying hydrated helps with digestion and overall well-being.

BALANCING PROTEIN AND CARBOHYDRATES

Achieving the right balance between protein and carbohydrates is crucial for maintaining energy levels and supporting your health goals. Here's how to strike that balance effectively:

UNDERSTAND PROTEIN NEEDS

Protein is essential for muscle repair, growth, and satiety. Aim to include a source of protein in every meal and snack. A general guideline is to consume about 0.8 to 1 gram of protein per kilogram of body weight. For example, a 150-pound person would need around 68-85 grams of protein per day. Adjust based on your activity level and specific goals.

LIMIT CARBOHYDRATES WISELY

On a low-carb diet, focus on reducing your intake of refined carbs and sugars while incorporating complex carbs in moderation. Include non-starchy vegetables like leafy greens, cauliflower, and zucchini. If you consume fruits, choose lower-carb options such as berries. Pay attention to portion sizes to keep your carb intake in check.

TRACK YOUR MACROS

Use a food diary or an app to track your protein and carbohydrate intake. This helps ensure you're meeting your goals and can adjust if needed. For instance, if you're finding yourself constantly hungry, you might need to increase your protein intake or adjust your carb sources.

LISTEN TO YOUR BODY

Everyone's needs are different. Pay attention to how you feel with different ratios of protein and carbs. If you're feeling sluggish or overly hungry, it might be worth tweaking your balance. Sometimes, small adjustments can make a big difference in how you feel and perform.

By structuring your meals thoughtfully and balancing protein and carbohydrates, you'll be able to maintain your energy levels, support muscle growth, and keep your cravings in check. This approach helps you stay aligned with your high-protein, low-carb lifestyle while enjoying a variety of satisfying and nutritious meals.

CHAPTER 2: 4-WEEK MEAL PLAN

WEEK 1

Day 1:

Breakfast: **Aesthetic Asparagus Frittata**

Lunch: **Power Pesto Chicken Pasta**

Snack: **Cranberry Protein Cookies**

Dinner: **Strength and Mass Meatloaf**

Total for the day:

Calories: **1610.00**; Protein: **110.00g**; Carbs: **75.00g**; Fat: **80.00g**

Day 2:

Breakfast: **Overnight Peanut Butter Protein Oats**

Lunch: **Baked Tamari Salmon and Zucchini**

Snack: **Tuna Salad Rice Cakes**

Dinner: **Strength and Mass Meatloaf**

Total for the day:

Calories: **1462.00**; Protein: **145.00g**; Carbs: **85.00g**; Fat: **63.00g**

Day 3:

Breakfast: **Aesthetic Asparagus Frittata**

Lunch: **Crispy Peanut Tofu with Cauliflower Rice**

Snack: **Tuna Salad Rice Cakes**

Dinner: **Power Pesto Chicken Pasta**

Total for the day:

Calories: **1584.00**; Protein: **92.00g**; Carbs: **79.00g**; Fat **85.00g**

Day 4:

Breakfast: **Overnight Peanut Butter Protein Oats**

Lunch: **Strength and Mass Meatloaf**

Snack: **Cranberry Protein Cookies**

Dinner: **Baked Tamari Salmon and Zucchini**

Total for the day:

Calories: **1431.00**; Protein: **132.00g**; Carbs: **82.00g**; Fat**64.00g**

Day 5:

Breakfast: **Aesthetic Asparagus Frittata**

Lunch: **Crispy Peanut Tofu with Cauliflower Rice**

Snack: **Cranberry Protein Cookies**

Dinner: **Strength and Mass Meatloaf**

Total for the day:

Calories: **1413.00**; Protein: **101.00g**; Carbs: **61.00g**; Fat: **86.00g**

Day 6:

Breakfast: **Salmon and Asparagus Omelet**

Lunch: **Power Pesto Chicken Pasta**

Snack: **Tuna Salad Rice Cakes**

Dinner: **Baked Tamari Salmon and Zucchini**

Total for the day:

Calories: **1808.00**; Protein: **293.00g**; Carbs: **144.00g**; Fat: **146.00g**

Day 7:

Breakfast: **Aesthetic Asparagus Frittata**

Lunch: **Baked Tamari Salmon and Zucchini**

Snack: **Cranberry Protein Cookies**

Dinner: **Power Pesto Chicken Pasta**

Total for the day:

Calories: **1566.00**; Protein: **105.00g**; Carbs: **64.00g**; Fat: **81.00g**

WEEK 2

Day 1:

Breakfast: **Sweet Potato Pancakes**

Lunch: **Mike's Savory Burgers**

Snack: **Stuffed Avocado**

Dinner: **Caribbean Turkey Thighs**

Total for the day:

Calories: **1991.00**; Protein: **163.00g**; Carbs: **198.00g**; Fat: **76.00g**

Day 2:

Breakfast: **Quinoa and Black Bean Casserole**

Lunch: **Caribbean Turkey Thighs**

Snack: **Flourless Chocolate Cake**

Dinner: **Sweet Potato Quesadillas**

Total for the day:

Calories: **1674.00**; Protein: **119.00g**; Carbs: **151.00g**; Fat: **75.00g**

Day 3:

Breakfast: **Sweet Potato Pancakes**

Lunch: **Mike's Savory Burgers**

Snack: **Protein Snack Box**

Dinner: **Taco Salad**

Total for the day:

Calories: **1693.00**; Protein: **143.00g**; Carbs: **139.00g**; Fat: **71.00g**

Day 4:

Breakfast: **Quinoa and Black Bean Casserole**

Lunch: **Sweet Potato Quesadillas**

Snack: **Stuffed Avocado**

Dinner: **Caribbean Turkey Thighs**

Total for the day:

Calories: **1746.00**; Protein: **118.00g**; Carbs: **208.00g**; Fat: **55.00g**

Day 5:

Breakfast: **Sweet Potato Pancakes**

Lunch: **Mike's Savory Burgers**

Snack: **Flourless Chocolate Cake**

Dinner: **Taco Salad**

Total for the day:

Calories: **1781.00**; Protein: **122.00g**; Carbs: **144.00g**; Fat: **79.00g**

Day 6:

Breakfast: **Quinoa and Black Bean Casserole**

Lunch: **Sweet Potato Quesadillas**

Snack: **Flourless Chocolate Cake**

Dinner: **Mike's Savory Burgers**

Total for the day:

Calories: **1615.00**; Protein: **96.00g**; Carbs: **156.00g**; Fat: **79.00**

Day 7:

Breakfast: **Sweet Potato Pancakes**

Lunch: **Caribbean Turkey Thighs**

Snack: **Flourless Chocolate Cake**

Dinner: **Taco Salad**

Total for the day:

Calories: **1840.00**; Protein: **135.00g**; Carbs: **140.00g**; Fat: **86.00g**

WEEK 3

Day 1:

Breakfast: Cottage Cheese Berry Bowl

Lunch: Brawny Chicken Chasseur

Snack: Honey Bread Pudding

Dinner: Seared Tuna and Corn Purée with Wasabi

Total for the day:

Calories: 1693.00; Protein: 204.00g; Carbs: 164.00g; Fat: 41.00g

Day 2:

Breakfast: Mighty Mini Meatloaves

Lunch: Thai Basil Chicken

Snack: Cheesecake In A Cup

Dinner: Curried Potatoes and Cauliflower

Total for the day:

Calories: 1166.00; Protein: 119.00g; Carbs: 84.00g; Fat: 44.00g

Day 3:

Breakfast: Cottage Cheese Berry Bowl

Lunch: Thai Basil Chicken

Snack: Honey Bread Pudding

Dinner: Brawny Chicken Chasseur

Total for the day:

Calories: 1623.00; Protein: 146.00g; Carbs: 154.00g; Fat: 41.00g

Day 4:

Breakfast: Mighty Mini Meatloaves

Lunch: Seared Tuna and Corn Purée with Wasabi

Snack: Cheesecake In A Cup

Dinner: Thai Basil Chicken

Total for the day:

Calories: 1226.00; Protein: 157.00g; Carbs: 42.00g; Fat: 47.00g

Day 5:

Breakfast: Cottage Cheese Berry Bowl

Lunch: Curried Potatoes and Cauliflower

Snack: Honey Bread Pudding

Dinner: Seared Tuna and Corn Purée with Wasabi

Total for the day:

Calories: 1681.00; Protein: 146.00g; Carbs: 206.00g; Fat: 49.00g

Day 6:

Breakfast: Mighty Mini Meatloaves

Lunch: Brawny Chicken Chasseur

Snack: Cheesecake In A Cup

Dinner: Seared Tuna and Corn Purée with Wasabi

Total for the day:

Calories: 1248.00; Protein: 167.00g; Carbs: 42.00g; Fat: 46.00g

Day 7:

Breakfast: Cottage Cheese Berry Bowl

Lunch: Thai Basil Chicken

Snack: Honey Bread Pudding

Dinner: Brawny Chicken Chasseur

Total for the day:

Calories: 1623.00; Protein: 146.00g; Carbs: 154.00g; Fat: 41.00g

WEEK 4

Day 1:

Breakfast: **Classic Steak, Mushroom and Eggs**

Lunch: **Slow Cooker Pork Roast**

Snack: **Black Bean Brownie Cups**

Dinner: **Cod, Pea and Spinach Risotto**

Total for the day:

Calories: **1765.00**; Protein: **134.00g**; Carbs: **152.00g**; Fat: **82.00g**

Day 2:

Breakfast: **Coconut and Macadamia French Toast**

Lunch: **Cod, Pea and Spinach Risotto**

Snack: **Apple-Cinnamon Flapjacks**

Dinner: **Sizzling Salmon Salad**

Total for the day:

Calories: **1449.00**; Protein: **143.00g**; Carbs: **191.00g**; Fat: **63.00g**

Day 3:

Breakfast: **Greek Yogurt Parfait**

Lunch: **Nourish Bowls**

Snack: **Black Bean Brownie Cups**

Dinner: **Slow Cooker Pork Roast**

Total for the day:

Calories: **1637.00**; Protein: **107.00g**; Carbs: **198.00g**; Fat: **68.00g**

Day 4:

Breakfast: **Classic Steak, Mushroom and Eggs**

Lunch: **Sizzling Salmon Salad**

Snack: **Apple-Cinnamon Flapjacks**

Dinner: **Cod, Pea and Spinach Risotto**

Total for the day:

Calories: **1817.00**; Protein: **160.00g**; Carbs: **151.00g**; Fat: **92.00g**

Day 5:

Breakfast: **Greek Yogurt Parfait**

Lunch: **Slow Cooker Pork Roast**

Snack: **Black Bean Brownie Cups**

Dinner: **Sizzling Salmon Salad**

Total for the day:

Calories: **1632.00**; Protein: **137.00g**; Carbs: **150.00g**; Fat: **90.00g**

Day 6:

Breakfast: **Coconut and Macadamia French Toast**

Lunch: **Cod, Pea and Spinach Risotto**

Snack: **Apple-Cinnamon Flapjacks**

Dinner: **Sizzling Salmon Salad**

Total for the day:

Calories: **1449.00**; Protein: **143.00g**; Carbs: **191.00g**; Fat: **63.00g**

Day 7:

Breakfast: **Greek Yogurt Parfait**

Lunch: **Nourish Bowls**

Snack: **Black Bean Brownie Cups**

Dinner: **Slow Cooker Pork Roast**

Total for the day:

Calories: **1637.00**; Protein: **107.00g**; Carbs: **198.00g**; Fat: **68.00g**

CHAPTER 3: BREAKFAST

AESTHETIC ASPARAGUS FRITTATA

Prep time: 10 minutes | **Cook time: 25 minutes** | **Serves 4**

- 2 cups of chopped asparagus
- ½ broccoli (florets only)
- 8 eggs
- handful of chopped parsley
- 1 tsp of chives
- 1 tbsp of olive oil
- 1 cup of low fat milk
- salt and pepper

1. Crack the eggs into a bowl, add the milk and some salt and pepper and whisk.
2. Get a covered skillet and steam the broccoli over a medium heat for 4-5 minutes. Set to one side.
3. Next, in the same skillet, heat the oil. Add the chopped asparagus, chopped parsley and chives into the skillet and cook for around 2-3 minutes on a medium heat.
4. Add the egg mixture, along with the broccoli into the skillet and cover the skillet evenly.
5. Cook for around 3-4 minutes or until the eggs are set right through
6. Take the skillet and place under the grill for around 2 minutes or until the top is golden (optional).
7. Plate up and serve.

Per Serving

Calories: 349 | **Protein: 23g** | **Carbs: 8g** | **Fat: 25g**

SWEET POTATO PANCAKES

Prep time: 10 minutes | **Cook time: 25 minutes** | **Serves 4**

- 1 medium sized sweet potato
- 1 egg
- 4 egg whites
- 8oz fat-free greek yogurt
- ½ cup of oats
- 1 tsp cinnamon
- 1 tsp vanilla extract
- 1 tsp of honey
- handful of diced strawberries
- handful of blueberries

1. Rinse sweet potato under cold water for a couple of seconds and then pierce it with a fork several times and place it in the microwave until soft (about 8 minutes).
2. After let it cool down before removing all skin with a knife.
3. Put the oats into a blender and blend until they are a fine powder, then place into a bowl.
4. Place the sweet potato in the blender and blend until smooth, and then mix with the powdered oats.
5. Add the egg, egg whites, vanilla, cinnamon, honey and yogurt and stir well. This is now your pancake batter.
6. Spray a pan with cooking spray and place over medium heat. Pour roughly a quarter of the batter into the pan and cook for 1-2 minutes. Flip the pancake and cook for another 30 seconds
7. Once done, remove your tasty pancake and top with the berries. 7. Use the same method for the rest of your batter.

Per Serving

Calories: 451 | **Protein: 38g** | **Carbs: 74g** | **Fat: 9g**

SCORE-BOARD SCOTCH EGGS

Prep time: **10 minutes** | Cook time: **25 minutes** | Serves **4**

- 16 oz lean ground chicken
- ½ tsp black pepper
- ½ tsp cayenne pepper
- ½ tsp paprika
- ½ tsp cloves
- ½ cup fresh parsley, finely chopped
- ½ tbsp dried chives
- 1 clove garlic, finely chopped
- 4 free range eggs, boiled and peeled

1. Preheat the oven to 375°F/190°C/Gas Mark 5.
2. Cover a baking sheet with parchment paper.
3. Combine the chicken with the paprika, cayenne pepper, pepper, cloves, chives, parsley and garlic in a mixing bowl and mix with your hands until thoroughly mixed.
4. Divide the mixture into 4 circular shapes with the palms of your hands.
5. Flatten each one into a pancake shape using the backs of your hands or a rolling pin.
6. Wrap the meat pancake around 1 egg, until it's covered. (You can moisten the meat with water first to help prevent it from sticking to your hands).
7. Bake in the oven for 25 minutes or until brown and crisp – check the meat is cooked through with a knife before serving.

Per Serving

Calories: **424** | Protein: **47g** | Carbs: **4g** | Fat: **22g**

COTTAGE CHEESE BERRY BOWL

Prep time: **5 minutes** | Cook time: **none** | Serves **4**

- 4 cups reduced-fat cottage cheese
- 6 cups raspberries, blueberries, or blackberries
- 4 tbsp. slivered or chopped almonds or walnuts
- 6 tbsp. unsweetened shredded coconut
- 6 tbsp. maple syrup

1. In a food processor, combine the cottage cheese and berries and pulse until mixed well.
2. Transfer to bowls to serve and top with the nuts, coconut, and a drizzling of maple syrup.

Per Serving

Calories: **888** | Fat: **30g** | Protein: **56g** | Carbs: **112g**

SALMON AND ASPARAGUS OMELET

Prep time: **10 minutes** | Cook time: **10 minutes** | Serves **1**

- 2 tsp. extra-virgin olive oil
- ½ small onion, diced
- 2 asparagus spears, cut into 1-inch pieces
- 1 (6-ounce) wild Pacific salmon fillet, cut into 1-inch cubes
- 1 clove garlic, minced
- 3 pitted Kalamata olives, sliced
- 1 tsp. capers
- 1 Roma tomato, diced
- Salt and ground black pepper, to taste
- 2 whole eggs, lightly beaten
- 4 egg whites, lightly beaten, or ¾ cup liquid egg white substitute

1. Add oil to a medium nonstick skillet and warm over medium-high heat. Add onion and asparagus, sautéing for 2 to 3 minutes. Stir in salmon pieces, lightly browning salmon pieces on all sides. Add garlic, olives, capers, and tomato; cook for another minute.
2. Add salt, pepper, whole eggs, and egg whites into the pan. Continually stir for about 1 minute, keeping the edges of the omelet from browning. Using a spatula, carefully flip omelet and cook for about 30 seconds. Serve immediately.

Per Serving

Calorie: **560** | Protein: **64 g** | Carbs: **13 g** | Fat: **28 g**

GREEK YOGURT PARFAIT

Prep time: **5 minutes** | Cook time: **15 minutes** | Serves **2**

- 2 cups nonfat plain greek yogurt
- 2 tbsp. creamy unsweetened peanut butter
- 1 tbsp. honey
- 1 tsp. vanilla extract
- 1 large banana, sliced
- ¼ cup granola

1. In a medium bowl, combine the yogurt, peanut butter, honey, and vanilla. Stir until completely combined and smooth.
2. Into each of 2 airtight storage containers, place a heaping cup of yogurt, topped with half a banana and 2 tbsp. of granola, and seal.

Per Serving

Calories: **343** | Fat: **16g** | Protein: **31g** | Carbs: **53g**

CLASSIC STEAK, MUSHROOM AND EGGS

Prep time: **5 minutes** | Cook time: **21 minutes** | Serves **2**

- 2x 6oz of rump beef steaks
- 1 tsp paprika
- 1 tsp mixed dried herbs
- 2 eggs
- 1 large beef tomato, sliced in half
- I large field mushroom, sliced in half

1. Heat the broiler on high.
2. Sprinkle paprika and herbs over each side of the steaks.
3. Add the steaks to a baking tray/griddle pan and place under the broiler.
4. Cook using the following approximate timings for each side: 2 minutes = rare ; 3-4 minutes = medium ; 5-6 minutes = well done.
5. Whilst the steak is cooking, add the tomato and mushroom to the pan, turning once through cooking.
6. Remove the steak and vegetables from the pan once done and allow to rest.
7. Crack the eggs onto the pan/tray and allow to cook for 4-5 minutes or until cooked through (3-4 minutes for a runny yolk and add a couple of minutes for a hard yolk).
8. Plate up and serve!

Per Serving

Calories: **470** | Protein: **60g** | Carbs: **6g** | Fat: **23g**

QUINOA AND BLACK BEAN CASSEROLE

Prep time: **15 minutes** | Cook time: **35 minutes** | Serves **4**

- 1 tsp. extra-virgin olive oil
- 1 medium onion, chopped
- 3 cloves garlic, peeled and minced
- 1 cup dry quinoa, rinsed
- 2 cups low-sodium vegetable broth
- 1 tsp. ground cumin
- ¼ tsp. ground cayenne pepper
- Salt and ground black pepper, to taste
- 1 cup frozen corn kernels
- 2 (15-ounce) cans black beans, rinsed and drained
- ½ cup chopped fresh cilantro

1. Warm oil in a large skillet over medium heat. Sauté onion and garlic, stirring occasionally, until lightly browned, about 10 minutes.
2. Stir quinoa and vegetable broth into the onion mixture. Season with cumin, cayenne, salt, and pepper. Bring the mixture to a boil.
3. Cover the pan with a lid and reduce the heat to low; simmer until quinoa is tender and broth is absorbed, about 20 minutes.
4. Stir corn and black beans into quinoa and continue to simmer until heated through, about 5 minutes. Garnish with cilantro and serve.

Per Serving

Calorie: **402** | Protein: **21 g** | Carbs: **77 g** | Fat: **5 g**

STRAWBERRY AND WALNUT YOGURT BOWL

Prep time: **5 minutes** | Cook time: **10 minutes** | Serves **1**

- 1 cup full-fat vanilla greek yogurt
- 2 tbsp. finely chopped walnuts
- ½ cup chopped strawberries
- ¼ tsp. ground cinnamon

1. Place ½ cup yogurt in a small bowl or Mason jar.
2. Top with 1 tbsp. walnuts, ¼ cup strawberries, and ¼ tsp. cinnamon. Layer remaining yogurt, walnuts, strawberries, and cinnamon on top.
3. Serve immediately or refrigerate, covered, overnight.

Per Serving

Calories: **292** | Fat: **17g** | Carbs: **13g** | Protein: **22g**

MIGHTY MINI MEATLOAVES

Prep time: **5 minutes** | Cook time: **30 minutes** | Serves **3**

- 1 cup lean ground turkey
- 1 cup skinless ground chicken
- 1 cup coconut milk
- 1 minced garlic clove
- ½ cup parsley
- 2 tbsp paprika
- Sprinkle of black pepper
- 2 tsp coconut oil

1. Preheat the oven to 400°F Gas Mark 6.
2. Mix turkey, chicken, garlic, parsley, paprika, and coconut milk together, mixing until the ingredients hold.
3. Season with black pepper to taste.
4. Line a muffin tin with coconut oil and divide the mixture into each hole.
5. Bake in the oven for 30 minutes or until the meat is cooked through.
6. Serve hot!

Per Serving

Calories: **459** | Protein: **53g** | Carbs: **2g** | Fat: **29g**

COCONUT AND MACADAMIA FRENCH TOAST

Prep time: **5 minutes** | Cook time: **10 minutes** | Serves **2**

French Toast

- ½ cup 2% milk
- 2 large eggs
- 2 egg whites or 6 tbsp. liquid egg white substitute
- 2 scoops vanilla protein powder
- ½ tsp. ground cinnamon
- 4 slices whole-grain bread

Topping

- 1 banana, peeled and sliced
- 2 tbsp. chopped macadamia nuts
- 2 tbsp. unsweetened coconut flakes

1. In a shallow dish, add milk, eggs, and egg whites, whisking together with a fork. Add protein powder and cinnamon, whisking again until completely mixed.
2. Soak a slice of bread in the mixture until soggy — letting it sit at least 30 seconds or so is ideal.
3. Coat a medium nonstick pan with cooking spray and warm on medium-high heat. Add 1 or 2 bread slices into the pan (no crowding the pan!) and cook until golden brown, about 2 minutes. Use a spatula to flip the slices, cooking again until firm, another 1 to 2 minutes. Transfer to a plate and repeat with remaining bread.
4. Meanwhile, in a small bowl, mix banana, nuts, and coconut flakes. Garnish each French toast piece with the topping. Serve.

Per Serving

Calorie: **102** | Protein: **43 g** | Carbs: **46 g** | Fat: **18 g**

OVERNIGHT PEANUT BUTTER PROTEIN OATS

Prep time: **5 minutes** | Cook time: **10 minutes** | Serves **2**

- 1 cup rolled oats
- ¼ cup vanilla protein powder
- ½ cup nonfat plain greek yogurt
- ¼ cup powdered peanut butter
- 1 ½ cups unsweetened almond milk

1. Combine all ingredients in a medium bowl. Divide mixture between two Mason jars or containers with lids.
2. Cover and refrigerate overnight.
3. Serve cold.

Per Serving

Calories: **354** | Fat: **8g** | Carbs: **41g** | Protein: **28g**

CHAPTER 4:
POULTRY

POWER PESTO CHICKEN PASTA

Prep time: 10 minutes | Cook time: 25 minutes | Serves 4

- 8 oz of chopped grilled chicken breast
- 1 cup of whole-wheat pasta
- 1 tbsp of pesto
- a pinch of black pepper
- handful of basil
- handful of spinach
- handful of rocket
- handful of pine nuts
- handful of diced tomatoes
- 2 tbsp of olive oil

1. Heat a large pan of water on high until it boils.
2. Add the whole-wheat pasta and leave until the water returns to boiling point.
3. Reduce the heat until the water simmers. Leave the whole-wheat pasta to cook for around 10 minutes.
4. Get a bowl and add the pesto, olive oil and black pepper and mix together.
5. Add the chopped chicken breast, pine nuts, tomatoes and herbs to the mixture.
6. Drain the pasta and fold the mix into the pan until the pasta is covered.

Per Serving

Calories: 550 | Protein: 25g | Carbs: 30g | Fat: 19g

THAI BASIL CHICKEN

Prep time: 5 minutes | Cook time: 15 minutes | Serves 4

- 4 (6-ounce) boneless, skinless chicken breasts, trimmed of fat
- 3 cloves garlic, peeled and minced
- 2 jalapeño peppers, minced
- 1 tbsp. fish sauce
- 1 tbsp. granulated sugar
- ¼ cup chopped fresh basil
- 1 tbsp. chopped fresh mint
- 1 tbsp. chopped unsalted dry-roasted peanuts

1. Cut each chicken breast into about 8 strips. Set aside.
2. Coat a large nonstick skillet with cooking spray and warm over medium-high heat. Add garlic and jalapeños. Sauté, stirring constantly, until garlic is just golden.
3. Add chicken strips and cook, stirring frequently, until chicken is fully cooked, about 8 to 10 minutes.
4. Add fish sauce and sugar. Sauté for 30 seconds and remove from heat. Garnish with basil, mint, and peanuts before serving.

Per Serving

Calorie: 220 | Protein: 40 g | Carbs: 5 g | Fat: 4 g

SLOW COOKER ITALIAN SLOPPY JOE

Prep time: **10 minutes** | Cook time: **4 hours 10 minutes** | Serves **4**

- 1 pound lean Italian turkey sausage, casings removed
- ½ cup chopped onion
- 3 cloves garlic, minced
- 1 red bell pepper, seeded and chopped in ½-inch pieces
- 1 green bell pepper, seeded and chopped in ½-inch pieces
- 1 1/3 cups canned crushed tomatoes
- ½ tsp. dried rosemary
- Salt and ground black pepper, to taste
- 4 whole-wheat 100-calorie potato rolls
- 4 slices reduced-fat provolone cheese
- 1 cup baby spinach

1. Warm a large nonstick skillet over medium-high heat. Add sausage, using a wooden spoon to break the meat into small pieces. Sauté for 5 to 6 minutes, stirring frequently, until the meat is cooked through.
2. Stir in onion and garlic. After cooking about 2 minutes, transfer sausage mixture to the slow cooker bowl. Add peppers, tomatoes, rosemary, salt, and pepper. Stir to combine.
3. Cover the slow cooker with a lid and set the heat to low. Cook for 4 hours.
4. To serve, fill a roll with a heaping ½ cup of meat. Top with cheese and baby spinach.

Per Serving

Calorie: **373** | Protein: **32 g** | Carbs: **31 g** | Fat: **15 g**

SOUTHWEST CHICKEN LETTUCE WRAPS

Prep time: **5 minutes** | Cook time: **10 minutes** | Serves **4**

- 1 pound ground chicken
- 1 cup cowboy caviar or salsa with black beans and corn
- 8 large soft leaves boston lettuce
- 3 tbsp. guacamole

1. Spray a medium skillet with nonstick cooking spray and heat over medium-high heat. Add ground chicken to the skillet. Sauté, using a wooden spoon to break up meat, until no pink remains, about 5 minutes.
2. Stir in Cowboy Caviar or salsa, reduce heat to medium-low, and cook for another 2 minutes.
3. Lay lettuce leaves on a flat surface. Fill each leaf with about ¼ cup chicken mixture and top with guacamole. Roll filled lettuce into cylinders and serve immediately.

Per Serving

Calories: **262** | Fat: **14g** | Carbs: **11g** | Protein: **24g**

MIGHTY MEXICAN CHICKEN STEW

Prep time: **5 minutes** | Cook time: **26 minutes** | Serves **4**

- 4 skinless chicken breasts
- 1 cup quinoa
- 16 oz of drained pinto beans
- 1 tbsp olive oil
- 1 chopped onion
- 2 chopped red peppers
- 3 tbsp chipotle paste
- 32 oz of tinned chopped tomatoes
- 2 chicken stock cubes
- Handful of chopped coriander
- 1 lime

1. Heat olive oil on a medium heat in a deep pan and add the onion and peppers and cook for 2-3 minutes.
2. Then add the chipotle paste and the tinned chopped tomatoes.
3. Add the chicken breast and add just enough water to cover the chicken by 1cm and then bring down the heat to let the mixture simmer. Cook for around 20 minutes until the chicken is cooked right through.
4. Add boiling water to a separate saucepan along with stock cubes. Pour in the quinoa and heat for around 12 minutes.
5. Add the pinto beans and cook for a further 3 minutes. Drain the quinoa and add in the coriander and squeeze the lime juice in - mix and place to one side.
6. Serve the chicken with the quinoa and cover with the tomato sauce from the pan.

Per serving

Calories: **464** | Protein: **51g** | Carbs: **53g** | Fat: **4g**

DECONSTRUCTED TURKEY LASAGNA

Prep time: **10 minutes** | Cook time: **20 minutes** | Serves **6**

- 20 ounces extra-lean ground turkey
- ½ tsp. salt, divided
- 8 ounces wide egg noodles
- 3 cups 15-Minute Marinara Sauce or store-bought
- ½ cup low-fat ricotta cheese
- ½ tsp. garlic powder
- ¼ tsp. freshly ground black pepper
- ½ cup shredded mozzarella cheese

1. Preheat the oven to 350°F.
2. In a large skillet over medium-high heat, crumble the turkey and cook for 5 to 6 minutes, until cooked through. Season with a ¼ tsp. of salt.
3. While the turkey is cooking, bring a large pot of water to a boil and cook the noodles according to the package directions. Drain.
4. Once the turkey is cooked, add the marinara sauce and mix well. Bring to a gentle simmer to heat through.
5. In a bowl, combine the noodles, ricotta cheese, garlic powder, remaining ¼ tsp. of salt, and pepper.
6. Place half of the noodles in a large baking dish; then top with half of the meat sauce. Add the remaining half of the noodles and then the remaining half of the meat sauce. Top with the mozzarella cheese and bake for 10 minutes, until the cheese is melted.

Per Serving

Calories: **402** | Fat: **9g** | Protein: **40g** | Carbs: **42g**

BRAWNY CHICKEN CHASSEUR

Prep time: 5 minutes | Cook time: 27 minutes | Serves 4

- 8 chopped rashers of turkey bacon
- 4 chopped chicken breasts
- 1 cup of baby mushrooms
- 1 tbsp plain flour
- 16oz of canned chopped tomatoes
- 1 beef stock cube
- 1 tbsp worcestershire sauce
- Handful of chopped parsley
- 1 tbsp olive oil

1. Heat the olive oil on a medium heat in a shallow saucepan and add the turkey bacon and cook for 4-5 minutes until it starts to brown.
2. Add the chopped chicken breasts and cook for around 5 minutes until golden. Increase the heat to high and add the baby mushrooms for 2 minutes. Add the flour and stir in until a paste starts to form.
3. Add the canned chopped tomatoes and beef stock cube to the saucepan and cook for around 10 minutes.
4. Then add the parsley and Worcestershire sauce to the pan, stir in and then serve.

Per Serving

Calories: **242** | Protein: **50g** | Carbs: **5g** | Fat: **3g**

CARIBBEAN TURKEY THIGHS

Prep time: 10 minutes | Cook time: 55 minutes | Serves 4

- 4x turkey thighs
- ¼ cup honey
- 1 tbsp mustard
- 2 tsp curry powder
- 1 garlic clove, minced
- 1 tbsp jamaican spice blend
- 1 lime
- 1 cup brown rice
- ½ cup canned kidney beans

1. Preheat the oven to 350°F.
2. Prepare marinade by mixing butter, honey, mustard, garlic and spices and pour over the chicken.
3. Add the turkey and the marinade to a baking dish and place in oven for 35-40 minutes.
4. Meanwhile prepare your rice by bringing a pan of water to the boil, add rice and beans.
5. Cover and simmer for 20 minutes.
6. Drain and cover the rice and return to the stove for 5 minutes.
7. When turkey is cooked through, serve on a bed of rice and beans and squeeze fresh lime juice over the top.
8. Enjoy.

Per Serving

Calories: **575** | Protein: **65g** | Carbs: **24g** | Fat: **22g**

CILANTRO CHICKEN AND AVOCADO BURRITOS

Prep time: **5 minutes** | Cook time: **10 minutes** | Serves **4**

- 4 (8") flour tortillas
- 1 pound boneless, skinless chicken breasts, cooked and shredded
- 1 medium avocado, peeled, pitted, and diced
- 1 cup shredded mexican-blend cheese
- 1 cup salsa verde
- ½ cup sour cream
- 4 tbsp. chopped fresh cilantro

1. Place tortillas on a work surface.
2. Equally distribute chicken, avocado, cheese, salsa, sour cream, and cilantro among tortillas.
3. Roll up tortillas and serve.

Per Serving

Calories: **425** | Fat: **22g** | Carbs: **20g** | Protein: **32g**

ARTICHOKE AND TOMATO CHICKEN BAKE

Prep time: **10 minutes** | Cook time: **25 minutes** | Serves **4**

- 4x skinless chicken thighs
- 1 onion, roughly chopped
- 2 garlic cloves, chopped
- 2 cans chopped tomatoes
- 1 tbsp balsamic vinegar
- ½ cup jarred artichokes
- 1 cup homemade chicken stock
- 1 bay leaf
- a pinch of black pepper
- 1 cup brown rice

1. Preheat oven to 375°F.
2. Add the onion, garlic, chopped tomatoes, artichoke, chicken stock, balsamic vinegar and the bay leaf to a baking dish and cover.
3. Place in the oven for 35-40 minutes or until chicken is thoroughly cooked.
4. Meanwhile add the rice to a pan of water and bring to the boil.
5. Lower the heat and simmer for 20 minutes or until most of the water is absorbed.
6. Drain, return the lid and steam for 5 minutes.
7. Plate up and serve with a pinch of black pepper and brown rice.

Per Serving

Calories: **695** | Protein: **49g** | Carbs: **55g** | Fat: **33g**

CHAPTER 5: RED MEAT AND PORK

ORANGE BEEF STIR-FRY

Prep time: 5 minutes | Cook time: 10 minutes | Serves 2

- ¼ cup orange marmalade
- 2 tbsp. low-sodium soy sauce or coconut aminos
- 1 tbsp. olive oil
- ½ pound lean sirloin steak, cut into thin strips
- 2 tsp. minced garlic
- 1 (14.4-ounce) bag frozen stir-fry vegetables (with broccoli), defrosted

1. In a small bowl, combine marmalade and soy sauce. Set aside.
2. Heat oil in large skillet over medium-high heat. Add steak to skillet and sauté for 2 minutes.
3. Add garlic, stir-fry vegetables, and marmalade mixture. Bring to a boil, stirring frequently.
4. Reduce heat to medium-low and simmer for 2–3 minutes until sauce thickens slightly.
5. Serve hot.

Per Serving

Calories: **392** | Fat: **13g** | Carbs: **40g** | Protein: **32g**

STRENGTH AND MASS MEATLOAF

Prep time: 10 minutes | Cook time: 25 minutes | Serves 4

- 36 oz of lean ground beef
- 1 tsp olive oil
- 1 chopped red onion
- 1 tsp garlic
- 3 chopped tomatoes
- 1 whole beaten egg
- 1cup of whole
- wheat bread crumbs
- handful of parsley
- ¼ cup of low fat parmesan
- ½ cup of organic skim milk
- a pinch of salt and pepper
- 1 tsp oregano

1. Preheat the oven to 400°F.
2. Add the oil to a pan and heat on a medium heat.
3. Cook the onions until soft but not browned. Remove the onions from the pan and let cool.
4. Get a big bowl and mix all of the ingredients together.
5. Put the meat in a big baking tray and cook on a high heat for around 30-35 minutes.
6. Serve once cooked through and piping hot.

Per Serving

Calories: **410** | Protein: **47g** | Carbs: **15g** | Fat: **19g**

FLANK STEAK WITH PAN-SEARED BRUSSELS SPROUTS

Prep time: 5 minutes, plus 1 hour to marinate | Cook time: 20 minutes | Serves 4

- 6 tbsp. extra-virgin olive oil
- 1½ tbsp. red wine vinegar
- 2 garlic cloves, minced
- 1½ tbsp. honey
- ¾ tsp. sea salt
- ¼ tsp. freshly ground black pepper
- 1 pound flank steak, sliced into strips
- nonstick cooking spray
- 1 pound brussels sprouts, halved

1. In a medium bowl, whisk together the olive oil, vinegar, garlic, honey, salt, and pepper.
2. Place the steak strips in a baking dish or bowl and top with two-thirds of marinade. Cover and chill for an hour.
3. Spray a large sauté pan or skillet with cooking spray and heat over medium-high heat. Add the Brussels sprouts and sauté 8 to 10 minutes, stirring frequently, until lightly brown. Pour the remaining marinade in the pan and cook just until the Brussels sprouts are coated and the sauce has reduced.
4. Divide the Brussels sprouts evenly among 4 containers.
5. Remove the steak from the marinade and place it in the pan (still on medium-high heat). Discard any extra marinade.
6. Pan fry for about 4 minutes per side, or until the steak is only slightly pink inside. Let cool.
7. In each container, place 4 ounces of steak strips on top of the Brussels sprouts.

Per Serving

Calories: **477** | Fat: **31g** | Protein: **36g** | Carbs: **17g**

SLOW COOKER PORK ROAST

Prep time: 5 minutes | Cook time: 6 to 8 hours | Serves 4

- 2 cups peeled and diced potatoes, any variety
- 3 cups peeled and chopped (2-inch pieces) carrots
- 1½ pounds boneless pork shoulder or butt roast
- ½ cup barbecue sauce
- 2 tbsp. honey
- ¼ cup chicken broth
- sea salt
- freshly ground black pepper

1. In a large slow cooker, scatter the potatoes and carrots in the bottom. Lay the pork on top of the vegetables, and pour the barbecue sauce, honey, and broth on top. Season with salt and pepper.
2. Set the slow cooker to high heat and cook for 6 to 8 hours.
3. Transfer the pork to a platter and shred using two large forks.
4. Into each of 4 airtight storage containers, place about 1¼ cups of vegetables and 6 ounces of pork. Spoon any additional liquid from the slow cooker on top and seal.

Per Serving

Calories: **465** | Fat: **19g** | Protein: **32g** | Carbs: **43g**

HIGH-PROTEIN ITALIAN PASTA BAKE

Prep time: **5 minutes** | Cook time: **10 minutes** | Serves **4**

- 4 ounces chickpea penne pasta
- 1 pound 90% lean ground beef
- 1 (16-ounce) bag frozen pepper and onion strips, thawed
- 2 tbsp. italian seasoning
- 1 cup marinara sauce
- 1 large egg
- 1 cup shredded mozzarella cheese

1. Preheat oven to 350°F.
2. Fill a large pot with water and bring to a boil over high heat. Add pasta and cook for 6 minutes. Drain and transfer to a large bowl.
3. Meanwhile, in a large skillet over medium-high heat, cook ground beef, breaking it up with a wooden spoon while it cooks. Sauté for 7–8 minutes until no longer pink. Add pepper and onion strips and Italian seasoning to the skillet and sauté 2 minutes.
4. Transfer ground beef mixture to the bowl with pasta. Add marinara sauce and egg. Mix ingredients well.
5. Pour ingredients into a 9" × 13" baking dish and top with cheese.
6. Bake for 10 minutes until cheese is melted. Serve immediately.

Per Serving

Calories: **438** | Fat: **21g** | Carbs: **24g** | Protein: **40g**

BEEF STROGANOFF

Prep time: **5 minutes** | Cook time: **20 minutes** | Serves **4**

- 10 ounces thick egg noodles
- 1 tsp. avocado oil
- 8 ounces mushrooms, sliced
- 20 ounces extra-lean ground beef
- 2 cups beef broth
- ½ cup low-fat sour cream
- ½ tsp. salt
- ¼ tsp. freshly ground black pepper

1. Bring a large pot of water to a boil. Cook the egg noodles according to the package directions. When softened, drain and rinse them under cold water to stop them from sticking.
2. Meanwhile, in a large skillet over medium heat, heat the oil. Add the mushrooms and cook for about 5 minutes, until browned and much of the liquid has evaporated.
3. Add the beef and cook for 5 minutes, until cooked through.
4. Add the broth and bring to a simmer for about 5 minutes. Stir in the sour cream, salt, and pepper.
5. Serve the beef on a bed of noodles.

Per Serving

Calories: **591** | Fat: **21g** | Protein: **44g** | Carbs: **54g**

FIT LAMB STEAKS WITH TZATZIKI

Prep time: **10 minutes** | Cook time: **25 minutes** | Serves **4**

- 2 x 5oz lean lamb steaks
- 1 tbsp fresh rosemary, finely chopped
- 1 tbsp extra virgin olive oil
- 1 lemon, juiced
- 1 tsp white wine vinegar
- ½ cup of low fat greek yogurt
- ¼ cucumber, chopped
- ¼ cup fresh mint
- ½ cup spinach
- 1 cup couscous
- ½ red onion, finely diced

1. Mix the olive oil with the rosemary and marinate the lamb steaks for as long as possible.
2. Heat a skillet over a medium to high heat and add the marinated steaks, cooking for 10 minutes on each side or until thoroughly cooked through.
3. Meanwhile, add the couscous to a heatproof bowl, pour boiling water over the top, cover and leave to steam for 5 minutes.
4. Stir through the diced red pepper and ½ lemon juice.
5. Mix the yogurt, ½ lemon juice, vinegar, mint and cucumber for your tzatziki. Season with a little salt and pepper.
6. Serve the lamb steaks with the couscous and tzatziki on the side.
7. Enjoy.

Per Serving

Calories: **403** | Protein: **40g** | Carbs: **25g** | Fat: **15g**

MIKE'S SAVORY BURGERS

Prep time: **5 minutes** | Cook time: **12 minutes** | Serves **4**

- 1 ½ pounds 92% lean ground beef
- 4 tbsp. Dijon mustard
- Salt and ground black pepper, to taste
- ½ cup low-carb ketchup
- ½ cup light mayonnaise
- 1 tbsp. red wine vinegar
- 2 tsp. Worcestershire sauce
- 4 whole-grain hamburger buns
- 4 sandwich slice pickles, halved

1. Prepare a grill to high heat. Lightly coat the grill grates with cooking spray.
2. In a large bowl, combine beef, mustard, salt, and pepper. Shape into 4 equal-sized patties and grill the patties for 5 to 6 minutes per side.
3. Meanwhile, in a small bowl, mix ketchup, mayonnaise, vinegar, and Worcestershire sauce.
4. Slice the buns in half and place cut side down on the grill to toast until light golden brown, about 10 seconds.
5. Place hamburgers onto buns and top with pickles and sauce. Serve.

Per Serving

Calorie: **516** | Protein: **42 g** | Carbs: **29 g** | Fat: **26 g**

29

PIZZA MEATBALLS

Prep time: **5 minutes** | Cook time: **10 minutes** | Serves **6**

- 1 ½ pounds 90% lean ground beef
- ⅓ cup italian bread crumbs
- ¼ cup grated parmesan cheese
- 1 large egg
- 1 tbsp. pizza seasoning (or 2 tsp. italian seasoning and 1 tsp. each garlic powder and onion salt)
- ½ tsp. salt
- ⅛ tsp. ground black pepper
- 1 pound mozzarella cheese, cut into 18 small cubes
- 2 (24-ounce) jars marinara sauce

1. Preheat oven to 375°F. Line a large baking sheet with parchment paper.
2. In a large bowl, combine ground beef, bread crumbs, Parmesan, egg, pizza seasoning, salt, and pepper. Mix well. Shape mixture into eighteen meatballs (1 ½"–2" in diameter) and place them on the prepared baking sheet.
3. Push a cube of mozzarella into the center of each meatball and reshape to completely enclose cheese.
4. Bake for 20 minutes.
5. Pour marinara sauce into a large saucepan and add meatballs. Bring to a boil over medium-high heat. Reduce heat to simmer 10–15 minutes until sauce is warm and meatballs are cooked all the way through.
6. Serve immediately, or store in an airtight container in the refrigerator for up to 1 week.

Per Serving

Calories: **620** | Fat: **35g** | Carbs: **28g** | Protein: **47g**

RAVIOLI LASAGNA

Prep time: **5 minutes** | Cook time: **10 minutes** | Serves **8**

- 1 pound pork sausage, casings removed
- 1 (26-ounce) jar pasta sauce, divided
- 2 (30-ounce) bags frozen large cheese ravioli, divided
- 1 (10-ounce) package frozen chopped spinach, thawed and drained
- 1 ½ cups shredded mozzarella cheese, divided
- ½ cup grated parmesan cheese, divided

1. Preheat oven to 350°F. Spray a 9" × 13" baking dish with nonstick cooking spray.
2. Place sausage in a large skillet over medium-high heat. Sauté until no longer pink, about 8 minutes, using a wooden spoon to break up meat as it cooks. Drain excess fat from skillet.
3. Spread one-third of pasta sauce on the bottom of the prepared dish.
4. Arrange one-half of ravioli on top of sauce. Top with sausage and spinach. Layer one-third of pasta sauce, ¾ cup mozzarella, and ¼ cup Parmesan over sausage and spinach, then arrange remaining ravioli on top.
5. Cover with the remaining sauce, mozzarella, and Parmesan. Tightly cover the baking dish with foil.
6. Bake 45 minutes. Uncover and bake for an additional 12–15 minutes or until cheese is melted and lightly browned. Serve immediately.

Per Serving

Calories: **694** | Fat: **38g** | Carbs: **56g** | Protein: **33g**

CHAPTER 6: FISH AND SEAFOOD

MIGHTY TUNA MELTS

Prep time: **10 minutes** | Cook time: **25 minutes** | Serves **4**

- 8 oz of tinned, drained tuna
- 2 chopped spring onions stems
- 4 tbsp low-fat mayonnaise
- 4 thick slices ezekial or wholemeal bread
- ½ cup grated low fat cheddar
- 2 tbsp of chilli flakes
- 1 squeezed lemon
- a pinch of salt and pepper

1. Toast the bread and pre-heat the grill.
2. Get a bowl and add the spring onions, mayonnaise, tuna and chilli flakes along with salt and pepper and the lemon juice. Mix everything together.
3. Spread the tuna mix over the top of the slices of bread and sprinkle the grated cheese over the top. Place under the grill until the cheese starts to bubble.
4. Plate up and serve.

Per Serving

Calories: **450** | Protein: **37g** | Carbs: **20g** | Fat: **24g**

BOURBON LIME SALMON

Prep time: **5 minutes** | Cook time: **45 minutes** | Serves **8**

- 1 cup packed brown sugar or brown sugar substitute
- 6 tbsp. bourbon
- ¼ cup soy sauce
- 2 tbsp. lime juice
- 2 tsp. freshly grated ginger
- ½ tsp. salt
- ¼ tsp. freshly
- ground black pepper
- 2 cloves garlic, crushed
- 8 (6-ounce) salmon fillets
- 4 tsp. sesame seeds
- ½ cup sliced green onions

1. Combine brown sugar, bourbon, soy sauce, lime juice, ginger, salt, pepper, and garlic in a large resealable plastic bag. Marinate salmon fillets in the bag at least 30 minutes in the refrigerator.
2. When ready to cook, preheat the broiler.
3. Transfer fish to broiler pan and discard marinade. Broil fish 10–12 minutes or until it flakes easily.
4. Sprinkle fish with sesame seeds and green onions and serve.

Per Serving:

Calories: **386.41** | Fat: **11.46 g** | Protein: **34.196 g** | Carbs: **28.96 g**

BAKED TAMARI SALMON AND ZUCCHINI

Prep time: 5 minutes | Cook time: 20 minutes | Serves 4

- 4 (6-ounce each) salmon fillets
- 2 zucchini, halved lengthwise and sliced into ½-inch matchsticks
- ¼ cup tamari sauce
- 2 tbsp. extra-virgin olive oil
- sea salt
- freshly ground black pepper

1. Preheat the oven to 415ºF.
2. Place the salmon fillets and zucchini slices on a baking sheet.
3. In a small bowl, mix together the tamari sauce and oil, and brush it over the salmon and zucchini. Sprinkle with salt and pepper.
4. Bake for 15 to 18 minutes, or until the salmon flakes apart when pierced with a fork. Remove from the oven and let cool.
5. Divide the zucchini among 4 airtight storage containers, place 1 salmon fillet in each, and seal.

Per Serving

Calories: **366** | Fat: **20g** | Protein: **42g** | Carbs: **4g**

SEARED TUNA AND CORN PURÉE WITH WASABI

Prep time: 10 minutes | Cook time: 30 minutes | Serves 4

- 1 ¾ cups water, plus more as needed
- 2 cups corn kernels cut from cobs (about 3 large ears), divided
- Salt, to taste
- 1 tsp. wasabi paste
- 4 (6-ounce) tuna steaks, about ¾-inch thick

1. In a small pot, combine water, 1 ½ cups corn, and salt. Bring to a boil over medium-high heat. Reduce the heat and simmer until corn is very soft, about 20 minutes. Transfer corn mixture to a blender and purée until smooth. Transfer puréed corn into a small bowl, add wasabi paste, and mix thoroughly.
2. Return the small pot over medium heat. Add remaining ½ cup corn and just enough water to cover it. Cook until corn is soft, about 10 minutes, and drain.
3. Meanwhile, season both sides of tuna with salt. Coat a large nonstick skillet with cooking spray and warm over medium-high heat. Once the pan is hot, sear each side of the tuna about 3 minutes each.
4. Add corn purée to each plate; top with corn kernels and seared tuna. Serve.

Per Serving

Calorie: **290** | Protein: **50 g** | Carbs: **15 g** | Fat: **4 g**

JACKET POTATO WITH TUNA

Prep time: **10 minutes** | Cook time: **25 minutes** | Serves **4**

- 1 large sweet potato
- 6 oz can tuna in olive oil, drained
- ½ finely chopped red onion,
- 1 small deseeded and chopped red chilli, (dried chilli will be just as good)
- 1 tbsp natural yoghurt
- a bunch of chopped spring onions

1. Preheat the oven to 400°F.
2. You don't need to peel the sweet potato but you may want to scrape off the nobly bits with a sharp knife!
3. Pierce the potato with a fork multiple times and place in the microwave for 20 minutes (if you don't have a microwave you can use the oven but it will take around 30 minutes).
4. Whilst it's cooking, mix the tuna with the chopped onion and chill and season with salt and pepper.
5. Place the sweet potato in the pre-heated oven for a further 5-10 minutes or until a little crispy and serve with the tuna mix and yoghurt over the top.
6. Sprinkle the chopped spring onion over that.

Per Serving

Calories: **352** | Protein: **33g** | Carbs: **27g** | Fat: **13g**

TUNA POWER WRAP

Prep time: **10 minutes** | Cook time: **none** | Serves **4**

- 2 cans water-packed tuna, drained
- 4 extra-large hard-boiled eggs, peeled and chopped
- 4 celery stalks, finely chopped
- ½ cup nonfat plain Greek yogurt
- ½ cup chopped red onion
- 2 tsp. whole-grain mustard
- Salt
- Freshly ground black pepper
- 4 large whole-grain tortillas
- 1 cup alfalfa sprouts
- 2 small ripe tomatoes, sliced

1. In a large bowl, break apart the tuna. Mix in the eggs, celery, yogurt, onion, and mustard. Season with salt and pepper.
2. Split the mixture between the tortillas and top with the alfalfa sprouts and tomatoes. Fold the sides in and roll the tortillas up.

Per Serving

Calories: **766** | Fat: **24g** | Protein: **64g** | Carbs: **76g**

CREAMY FETTUCINE WITH SCALLOPS

Prep time: **10 minutes** | Cook time: **25 minutes** | Serves **5**

- Salt and ground black pepper, to taste
- 8 ounces whole-grain fettuccine
- 1 pound large sea scallops
- 1 (8-ounce) bottle clam juice (the lowest sodium available)
- 1 cup 2% milk
- 3 tbsp. cornstarch
- 3 cups frozen peas
- ? cup chopped chives
- ½ tsp. lemon zest
- 1 tsp. lemon juice
- ½ cup grated Parmesan cheese

1. Bring a large pot of lightly salted water to a boil over high heat. Cook fettuccine according to package instructions. Drain the pasta and reserve.
2. Meanwhile, dry scallops with a paper towel and sprinkle with salt. Coat a large nonstick skillet with cooking spray and warm over medium-high heat. Add scallops and cook until golden brown, about 2 to 3 minutes per side. Remove from pan and reserve.
3. Add clam juice to the pan. In a medium bowl, add milk, cornstarch, salt, and pepper; whisk until smooth. Pour milk mixture into the pan and whisk with clam juice. Once the mixture is simmering, stir constantly until sauce thickens, about 1 to 2 minutes.
4. Add reserved scallops and peas to clam sauce and bring to a simmer. Stir in reserved fettuccine, chives, lemon zest, lemon juice, and most of the cheese; mix well. Remove pan from the heat and top pasta with remaining cheese. Serve.

Per Serving

Calorie: 402 | **Protein: 31 g** | **Carbs: 56 g** | **Fat: 5 g**

COD, PEA AND SPINACH RISOTTO

Prep time: **10 minutes** | Cook time: **25 minutes** | Serves **4**

- 2x smoked cod fillets skinless, boneless
- 1 tbsp extra virgin olive oil
- 1 white onion, finely diced
- 2 cups brown rice
- 4 cups vegetable stock
- 1 cup fresh spinach
- leaves
- 1 cup of frozen peas
- 3 tbsp low fat greek yogurt (optional)
- a pinch of black pepper
- 4 lemon wedges
- 1 cup of arugula

1. Heat the oil in a large pan on a medium heat.
2. Sauté the chopped onion for 5 minutes until soft before adding in the rice and
3. stirring for 1-2 minutes.
4. Add half of the stock and stir slowly.
5. Slowly add the rest of the stock whilst continuously stirring for up to 20-30 minutes (this is a bit of a workout!)
6. Stir in the spinach and peas to the risotto.
7. Place the fish on top of the rice, cover and steam for 10 minutes.
8. Use your fork to break up the fish fillets and stir into the rice with the yogurt.
9. Sprinkle with freshly ground pepper to serve and a squeeze of fresh lemon.
10. Garnish with the lemon wedges and serve with the arugula.

Per Serving

Calories: **527** | Protein: **34g** | Carbs: **74g** | Fat: **12g**

GARLIC AND HERB SEARED SALMON

Prep time: **5 minutes** | Cook time: **5 minutes** | Serves **4**

- 4 cloves garlic, crushed
- 1 tsp. dried Herbes de Provence
- 1 tsp. red wine vinegar
- 2 tbsp. plus 1 tsp. olive oil, divided
- 2 tbsp. Dijon mustard
- 4 (6-ounce) wild-caught salmon fillets
- 4 lemon wedges for serving

1. Combine garlic, herbs, vinegar, 1 tsp. oil, and mustard in a food processor until smooth.
2. Heat remaining 2 tbsp. of oil in a large nonstick skillet over medium-high heat and grill salmon fillets 5 minutes.
3. Flip fillets and cook 3 minutes, spooning half the garlic sauce on the cooked side of each fillet.
4. Flip fillets again, cooking 1 more minute and spreading sauce on the other side of fillets. Flip fillets one last time and cook 1 minute.
5. Remove and serve each fillet with a fresh lemon wedge.

Per Serving

Calories: **258.78** | Fat: **12.1g** | Protein: **33.8 g** | Carbs: **1.4 g**

CHAPTER 7: VEGETARIAN SIDES AND SOUPS

RICE AND PEAS

Prep time: 10 minutes | Cook time: 25 minutes | Serves 4

- 2 cups brown rice
- 2 tbsp. olive oil
- 8 oz dried kidney beans
- 1 tsp chilli powder

1. Soak the kidney beans in water overnight (you can buy tinned and use immediately if you're in a rush but you won't get that authentic color or taste!)
2. Boil the liquid with the kidney beans in using a large saucepan on a high heat (add water if you need to).
3. Add the rice and cook for 30 minutes and then drain. Keep the rice in the pan, add the kidney beans and cover and steam for 4 minutes.
4. Sprinkle chilli powder over your rice and serve.

Per Serving

Calories: 430 | Protein: 20g | Carbs: 16g | Fat: 15g

GARLIC CHEDDAR CAULIFLOWER SOUP

Prep time: 5 minutes | Cook time: 10 minutes | Serves 2

- 2 tbsp. olive oil
- 1 small yellow onion, peeled and chopped
- 2 cloves garlic, peeled and minced
- 1 medium head cauliflower, cored, outer leaves removed, and chopped
- 4 cups low-sodium chicken broth
- ½ cup shredded sharp cheddar cheese
- ¼ cup grated parmesan cheese

1. Heat oil in a large saucepan over medium heat. Sauté onion and garlic 5 minutes.
2. Add cauliflower and broth. Increase heat to high and bring to a boil.
3. Reduce heat to medium-low and simmer 20 minutes until cauliflower is soft.
4. Remove from heat, then transfer soup to a blender and process until smooth (or use a handheld blender).
5. Return soup to pot, stir in Cheddar and Parmesan, and heat, stirring constantly, over medium heat 5 minutes until cheeses melt. Serve hot.

Per Serving

Calories: 351 | Fat: 23g | Carbs: 18g | Protein: 18g

SWEET POTATO QUESADILLAS

Prep time: 5 minutes | **Cook time: 10 minutes** | **Serves 4**

- 1 large sweet potato, peeled and sliced
- ¼ tsp. salt
- ¼ tsp. ground black pepper
- 4 (7") whole-grain tortillas
- ⅔ cup canned black beans, drained and rinsed
- 1 cup chopped baby spinach
- 1 ½ cups shredded cheddar cheese

1. Preheat oven to 400°F. Line a baking sheet with parchment paper.
2. Fill a medium saucepan with 1" of water and bring to a boil over high heat. Place sweet potato in a steaming basket and place basket in the saucepan. Cover and steam for 10–12 minutes until tender. Transfer sweet potatoes to a bowl and mash with a fork. Season with salt and pepper.
3. Lay 2 tortillas on the prepared baking sheet and spread with mashed sweet potato. Top with black beans, spinach, and cheese. Cover with the remaining tortillas and bake for 10–15 minutes until golden brown and crispy.
4. Slice into wedges and serve.

Per Serving

Calories: 320 | **Fat: 14g** | **Carbs: 36g** | **Protein: 14g**

MUSCLE LENTIL SOUP

Prep time: 10 minutes | **Cook time: 25 minutes** | **Serves 4**

- ⅓ cup of vegetable broth
- 1 tsp of olive oil
- 1 carrot, sliced
- 4 oz of brown lentils
- 1 onion, diced
- 2 tsp of lemon juice
- 2 bay leaves
- salt and pepper, to taste
- ¼ tsp of dried thyme

1. Sauté carrot and onion in sunflower oil on a medium heat for around 5 minutes or until onions have become translucent.
2. Add lentils, bay leaves, thyme, salt and pepper, and vegetable broth. Lower heat and simmer. Put the lid on and allow to cook for about 40 to 45 minutes, just to make sure the lentils have softened.
3. Take the leaves out, and stir the lemon juice in.
4. Serve hot.

Per Serving

Calories: 398 | **Protein: 25g** | **Carbs: 70g** | **Fat: 2g**

FISH AND VEGETABLE S OUP

Prep time: 10 minutes | Cook time: 15 minutes | Serves 4

- 1 lb. firm fresh white fish fillets of any white fish of your choice
- 1 tbsp. butter
- ¼ cup chopped onion
- 1 clove of garlic
- 3 ½ cups chicken broth
- 1 cup carrots
- 1 cup frozen cut green beans
- ½ cup frozen corn
- ½ tsp. salt
- ½ tsp. dried basil leaves
- ¼ tsp. dried oregano leaves
- ⅛ tsp. pepper

1. Preheat soup pot to medium heat.
2. Thinly chop carrots, onions, and garlic.
3. Melt butter in the soup pot and add onions and garlic.
4. Stir until garlic is brown.
5. Add every other ingredient except fish and bring to a boil, stirring throughout.
6. Lower heat to a simmer and cook for eight minutes.
7. Add fish and cook uncovered for another seven minutes until fish flakes, stirring occasionally.
8. Serve into bowls and enjoy!

Per Serving

Calories: **190** | Fat: **5g** | Carbs: **11g** | Protein: **25g**

CURRIED POTATOES AND CAULIFLOWER

Prep time: 5 minutes | Cook time: 25 minutes | Serves 4

- Salt, to taste
- 1 (2- to 3-pound) head cauliflower, cut into florets
- 1 pound potatoes, peeled and cut into 1-inch cubes
- 1 medium onion, chopped
- 2 cloves garlic, peeled and minced
- 2 tbsp. garam masala or curry powder
- 1 cup low-sodium vegetable broth
- 2 cups frozen peas

1. Bring a pot of lightly salted water to a boil over high heat. Add the cauliflower and potatoes; cook for 4 to 5 minutes and drain.
2. Meanwhile, coat a Dutch oven with cooking spray and warm over medium heat. Add chopped onion and garlic and cook until onion softens, about 2 to 3 minutes. Add garam masala and stir for 1 minute.
3. Transfer cooked potatoes and cauliflower to the Dutch oven. Stir well, coating in the onion mixture. Add broth and deglaze the pan.
4. Cover with a lid and let mixture simmer for 10 minutes. Stir in peas, cover, and cook for another 5 to 7 minutes. Serve immediately.

Per Serving

Calorie: **230** | Protein: **12 g** | Carbs: **47 g** | Fat: **1g**

CRISPY PEANUT TOFU WITH CAULIFLOWER RICE

Prep time: 5 minutes | Cook time: 10 minutes | Serves 2

- 1 ½ tsp. sesame oil
- 1 ½ tbsp. low-sodium soy sauce or coconut aminos
- 2 tsp. maple syrup
- 1 ½ tbsp. creamy peanut butter
- 8 ounces extra-firm tofu, drained, cut into cubes, and patted dry
- 2 tsp. olive oil
- 2 tsp. cornstarch
- ½ tsp. salt
- 2 cups riced cauliflower
- ½ small lime, sliced into wedges

1. Preheat oven to 400°F. Line a baking sheet with parchment paper.
2. In a large mixing bowl, whisk together sesame oil, soy sauce, maple syrup, and peanut butter. Set aside.
3. Place tofu in a large mixing bowl and toss with olive oil, cornstarch, and salt. Transfer to the prepared baking sheet.
4. Bake for 15–20 minutes until edges begin to brown and crisp.
5. Add tofu to the mixing bowl with the peanut butter mixture and toss to coat.
6. Heat a medium nonstick skillet over medium heat. Add riced cauliflower and cook for 5–6 minutes until warm.
7. Top with tofu and serve immediately with lime wedges.

Per Serving

Calories: 353 | Fat: 25g | Carbs: 16g | Protein: 16g

SAUSAGE AND KALE SOUP

Prep time: 5 minutes | Cook time: 10 minutes | Serves 4

- 12 ounces pork sausage, sliced
- 1 medium yellow onion, peeled and diced
- 2 medium carrots, peeled and diced
- 2 stalks celery, diced
- 8 cups chopped kale leaves
- 8 cups low-sodium chicken broth
- 1 tbsp. salt
- ¾ cup brown rice

1. Combine all ingredients in a 6- to 8-quart slow cooker and cook on high for 4 hours or on low for 8 hours. Serve hot.

Per Serving

Calories: 626 | Fat: 39g | Carbs: 35g | Protein: 32g

NOURISH BOWLS

Prep time: **5 minutes** | Cook time: **10 minutes** | Serves **2**

- ½ tbsp. avocado oil
- ½ medium sweet onion, peeled and chopped
- 1 cup white beans, drained and rinsed
- 2 cups baby spinach
- ⅛ tsp. salt
- ⅛ tsp. ground black pepper
- 2 cups cooked brown rice
- 2 tbsp. dried cranberries
- 2 tbsp. pumpkin seeds
- ¼ cup Cinnamon Tahini Dressing

1. Heat oil in a large skillet over medium-high heat and sauté onion for 2–3 minutes until slightly softened.
2. Add beans and spinach and heat for 1 minute until spinach is wilted. Season with salt and pepper. Remove from heat and stir in rice.
3. Add cranberries, pumpkin seeds, and dressing. Gently stir to combine. Serve immediately.

Per Serving

Calories: **526** | Fat: **15g** | Carbs: **73g** | Protein: **26g**

CUMIN-SPIKED BLACK BEAN SOUP

Prep time: **15 minutes** | Cook time: **55 minutes** | Serves **2**

- 2 tsp. extra-virgin olive oil
- 1 small onion, finely chopped
- 1 carrot, peeled and chopped
- 2 celery stalks, chopped
- ½ jalapeño pepper, seeded and chopped
- 2 cloves garlic, minced
- 1 tsp. ground cumin
- 1 bay leaf
- 4 cups low-sodium chicken broth
- 1 (14.5-ounce) can black beans, drained and rinsed
- 2 tsp. red wine vinegar
- Chopped fresh cilantro, to taste
- Salt and ground black pepper, to taste

1. In a medium pot, warm olive oil over medium-high heat. Add the onion and sauté for about 3 minutes.
2. Add carrot, celery, and jalapeño; sauté for about 5 minutes. Stir in garlic, cumin, and bay leaf, and sauté for about 30 seconds. Add chicken broth and black beans. Bring soup to a simmer and reduce heat to low; cook until flavors have melded together, about 30 to 45 minutes.
3. To serve, remove bay leaf. Stir in red wine vinegar and cilantro; season with salt and pepper. Serve immediately.

Per Serving

Calorie: **309** | Protein: **20 g** | Carbs: **47 g** | Fat: **5 g**

CHAPTER 8:
SALADS

STEAK AND BALSAMIC SPINACH SALAD

Prep time: **10 minutes** | Cook time: **25 minutes** | Serves **4**

- 8 oz frying beef steak
- 1 chopped red onion
- 1 tsp of crushed garlic
- ¼ cup baby spinach
- ¼ cup watercress
- 4 cherry tomatoes, halved
- 2 tbsp of balsamic vinegar
- 2 tbsp olive oil
- sprinkle of salt and pepper

1. Sprinkle salt and pepper over steak.
2. Add a tbsp of olive oil to a griddle pan and heat on a high temperature.
3. Place the steak in the pan and cook for 8 minutes in total, turning the steak half way through.
4. Remove the steak from the pan and rest for 3 minutes.
5. Cut it into 2cm strips.
6. Get a bowl and add the chopped tomatoes, watercress, baby spinach, garlic and onions.
7. Place the steak strips in the bowl along with the vinegar and a tbsp of olive oil. Mix together.
8. Plate up and serve.

Per Serving

Calories: **308** | Protein: **34g** | Carbs: **15g** | Fat: **14g**

CHICKEN AND KALE CAESAR SALAD

Prep time: **5 minutes** | Cook time: **10 minutes** | Serves **4**

- ¼ cup grated parmesan cheese
- ¼ cup nonfat plain greek yogurt
- ¼ cup lemon juice
- ½ tsp. worcestershire sauce
- 3 tbsp. olive oil, divided
- 1 tsp. minced garlic
- 1 pound boneless, skinless chicken breasts
- ½ tsp. salt
- ½ tsp. ground black pepper
- 4 cups trimmed and chopped kale

1. Combine cheese, yogurt, lemon juice, Worcestershire sauce, 2 tbsp. oil, and garlic in a food processor and pulse until combined. Set aside.
2. Season chicken with salt and pepper.
3. Heat remaining 1 tbsp. oil in a large skillet over medium heat.
4. Place chicken in skillet and cook 6–8 minutes per side until no longer pink. Remove from skillet and set aside to cool for 5 minutes.
5. Place chicken in a large bowl and shred, using two forks. Add kale and dressing. Toss to coat.
6. Divide mixture among four bowls and serve.

Per Serving

Calories: **280** | Fat: **13g** | Carbs: **9g** | Protein: **33g**

TROPICAL CHICKEN SALAD WITH PINEAPPLE AND PECANS

Prep time: 25 minutes | Cook time: none | Serves 1

- 1 (6-ounce) boneless, skinless chicken breast, cooked and cubed
- 2 tbsp. chopped celery
- ¼ cup chopped pineapple
- ¼ cup peeled orange segments
- 1 tbsp. chopped pecans
- ¼ cup halved seedless grapes
- Salt and ground black pepper, to taste
- 2 cups torn romaine lettuce

1. In a medium bowl, add chicken, celery, pineapple, oranges, pecans, and grapes. Gently mix together with a spoon until combined and season with salt and pepper.
2. On a plate, make a bed of lettuce. Top with the chicken mixture and serve.

Per Serving

Calorie: 323 | Protein: 42 g | Carbs: 22 g | Fat: 9 g

ANTIPASTO PASTA SALAD

Prep time: 10 minutes | Cook time: 15 minutes | Serves 8

- 8 cups chopped romaine lettuce
- ¾ cup grape or cherry tomatoes, halved
- 6 oz. provolone cheese
- 4 oz. canned marinated artichokes hearts
- ½ cup black olives
- 2 oz. salami, diced
- 2 oz. pepperoni, quartered
- ¼ cup sliced pepperoncinis
- ¼ cup sliced red onion

Recommended Dressing:
- Macro Italian Dressing

1. Drain the artichoke hearts and olives in separate strainers to remove excess liquid.
2. Rinse the romaine lettuce
3. Chop the provolone cheese into bite-size chunks.
4. Toss all directions in a large bowl with chosen dressing.
5. Serve and enjoy!

Per Serving

Calories: 157 | Fat: 4g | Carbs: 3g | Protein: 9g

SIZZLING SALMON SALAD

Prep time: **10 minutes** | Cook time: **25 minutes** | Serves **4**

- 6 oz fillet salmon
- 6 cherry tomatoes
- 1 cup of couscous
- 3 stems of asparagus (chop off the very end of the base but leave the rest intact)
- 2 oz of diced low-fat mozzarella cheese
- 1 bell pepper sliced
- 1 tbsp balsamic vinegar
- 1 tbsp olive oil
- a pinch of salt and pepper

1. Preheat the grill.
2. Layer the couscous with boiling water from the kettle (about 1cm over the top of the couscous, cover and leave to steam)
3. Grill salmon for 10-15 minutes or until cooked through. Place to one side.
4. Uncover the couscous and stir through with a fork to break up the grains.
5. Now just add your pepper, mozzarella and halved cherry tomatoes to the couscous.
6. You will need to grill your asparagus for 3-4 minutes, turning every so often until lightly browned around the surface.
7. Once the asparagus is ready, place it along with the salmon on the bed of couscous and drizzle with olive oil and balsamic vinegar.
8. Salt and pepper to taste.

Per Serving

Calories: **521** | Protein: **46g** | Carbs: **24g** | Fat: **27g**

ROASTED BUTTERNUT SQUASH AND CHICKPEA LOADED KALE SALAD

Prep time: **10 minutes** | Cook time: **20 minutes** | Serves **2**

- Nonstick cooking spray
- 1 (15-ounce) can chickpeas, drained and rinsed
- 4 ounces extra-firm tofu, pressed and chopped into 1-inch cubes
- 1 cup chopped frozen or fresh butternut squash
- ½ tsp. salt
- ¼ tsp. freshly ground black pepper
- 3 cups chopped, stemmed kale
- ¼ cup pepitas
- ¼ cup Parsley, Garlic, and Sunflower Seed Sauce or Balsamic Vinaigrette

1. Preheat the oven to 425°F and place a baking sheet in the oven.
2. When the oven is preheated, remove the sheet from the oven and coat with cooking spray. Pour the chickpeas, tofu, and butternut squash onto the baking sheet and coat lightly with cooking spray. Season with the salt and pepper.
3. Bake for 20 minutes, stirring once or twice, until browned and tender.
4. In a large bowl, toss the chickpeas mixture with the kale. Sprinkle with the pepitas and drizzle with the sauce to serve.

Per Serving

Calories: **464** | Fat: **21g** | Protein: **25g** | Carbs: **50g**

MACRO COBB SALAD

Prep time: 10 minutes | Cook time: 15 minutes | Serves 1

- 2 cups chopped Romaine lettuce
- 1 hard-boiled egg
- ¼ avocado
- 1 rotisserie chicken breast
- 1 oz. applewood
- smoked ham (chopped)
- ½ cup chopped cucumber
- ½ cup chopped tomatoes

Dressing Recommendation:

- Dijon Vinaigrette

1. Chop the chicken and avocado to bite-size slices, making sure to remove the bones and skin from the chicken.
2. Mix all the directions on a plate.
3. Serve with chosen dressing and enjoy!

Per Serving

Calories: **478** | Fat: **4g** | Carbs: **1g** | Protein: **78g**

TURKEY-APPLE-WALNUT KALE SALAD

Prep time: 10 minutes | Cook time: 15 minutes | Serves 2

- 4 cups chopped kale
- ½ avocado, cubed
- ¼ red onion, finely chopped
- ¼ cup blueberries
- 2 tbsp. chopped and toasted
- walnuts
- ½ medium apple, cubed
- 8 ounces roasted turkey, sliced
- 6 tbsp. Greek Yogurt and Honey Dressing

1. In a medium bowl, combine the kale and avocado and massage the avocado into the kale with your hands. Add the onion, blueberries, walnuts, apple, and turkey, and toss well.
2. In each of 2 airtight storage containers or jars, place about 2 cups of salad. In 2 small airtight storage containers, place 3 tbsp. of Greek Yogurt and Honey Dressing. To serve, mix the salad and dressing.

Per Serving

Calories: **419** | Fat: **13g** | Protein: **44g** | Carbs: **34g**

ASIAN SALMON SALAD

Prep time: 5 minutes | Cook time: 10 minutes | Serves 4

- 2 tbsp. low-sodium soy sauce
- 1 (1") piece ginger, peeled and chopped
- 1 clove garlic, peeled and minced
- 2 tbsp. chopped scallions
- ¼ cup vegetable oil
- 3 tbsp. white vinegar
- 1 tbsp. sesame oil
- 1 tbsp. olive oil
- 4 (6-ounce) salmon fillets
- 2 tsp. salt
- 2 tsp. ground black pepper
- 4 cups mixed salad greens

1. Combine soy sauce, ginger, garlic, scallions, vegetable oil, vinegar, and sesame oil in a food processor and pulse until smooth.
2. Heat olive oil in a large skillet over medium heat. Season salmon with salt and pepper and cook 5 minutes per side.
3. Divide greens among four bowls. Top with salmon and drizzle with dressing before serving.

Per Serving

Calories: 543 | Fat: 38g | Carbs: 4g | Protein: 45g

TACO SALAD

Prep time: 5 minutes | Cook time: 10 minutes | Serves 4

- 1 pound 90% ground beef
- 2 tbsp. taco seasoning
- 1 cup salsa with black beans and corn
- 2 heads romaine hearts, chopped
- 1 cup chopped cherry tomatoes
- ½ cup guacamole
- 1 cup shredded sharp cheddar cheese

1. Place beef in a medium skillet over medium-high heat. Using a wooden spoon, break meat into very small pieces and cook until no longer pink, about 8 minutes. Drain any excess fat from beef.
2. Add taco seasoning and salsa to beef and stir to combine. Stir and heat over medium heat for 3 minutes.
3. Place lettuce on four plates and top evenly with beef mixture, tomatoes, guacamole, and cheese. Serve immediately.

Per Serving

Calories: 437 | Fat: 21g | Carbs: 27g | Protein: 33g

SALMON AVOCADO NICOISE SALAD

Prep time: 20 minutes | Cook time: 15 minutes | Serves 4

- 4 salmon fillets
- 1 can black olives, drained and halved
- 2 hard-boiled eggs, quartered
- ½ cup green beans, cooked and chopped
- 1 ripe avocado, cubed
- 2 tbsp. red wine vinegar
- 1 tbsp. Dijon mustard
- 2 tbsp. olive oil
- Salt and pepper to taste

1. Season salmon fillets with salt and pepper. Grill or bake until cooked through. Let cool, then flake into pieces.
2. In a large bowl, combine black olives, hard-boiled eggs, green beans, and avocado.
3. In a small bowl, whisk together red wine vinegar, Dijon mustard, and olive oil. Season with salt and pepper.
4. Pour dressing over salad and toss to coat.
5. Top with flaked salmon and serve immediately.

Per Serving

Calories: 380 | Protein: 30g | Carbs: 10g | Fat: 22g

GRILLED CHICKEN CAESAR SALAD

Prep time: 15 minutes | Cook time: 20 minutes | Serves 4

- 2 boneless, skinless chicken breasts
- 1 head romaine lettuce, chopped
- ½ cup grated Parmesan cheese
- 4 slices crispy bacon, crumbled
- ¼ cup croutons
- 2 cloves garlic, minced
- ¼ cup lemon juice
- ¼ cup olive oil
- 1 tsp. Dijon mustard
- Salt and pepper to taste

1. Season chicken breasts with salt and pepper. Grill or pan-fry until cooked through. Let cool, then slice into strips.
2. In a large bowl, combine romaine lettuce, Parmesan cheese, bacon, and croutons.
3. In a small bowl, whisk together garlic, lemon juice, olive oil, Dijon mustard, salt, and pepper.
4. Pour dressing over salad and toss to coat.
5. Top with grilled chicken and serve immediately.

Per Serving

Calories: 420 | Protein: 35g | Carbs: 12g | Fat: 25g

CHAPTER 9: SNACKS AND DESSERTS

BROILED GRAPEFRUIT WITH GREEK YOGURT AND PECANS

Prep time: **5 minutes** | Cook time: **10 minutes** | Serves **2**

- 2 grapefruit, halved
- 4 packed tbsp. brown sugar
- 2 cups nonfat plain Greek yogurt
- ¼ cup pecan pieces
- 2 tbsp. honey

1. Preheat the broiler on high.
2. Place the grapefruit, cut-side up, on a baking sheet and sprinkle each half with 1 tbsp. of brown sugar.
3. Broil for about 10 minutes, until the sugar caramelizes and is bubbling. Top each half with ½ cup of yogurt, 1 tbsp. of pecan pieces, and ½ tbsp. of honey. Serve warm.

Per Serving

Calories: **515** | Fat: **11g** | Protein: **28g** | Carbs: **82g**

CRANBERRY PROTEIN COOKIES

Prep time: **5 minutes** | Cook time: **10 minutes** | Makes **8 cookies**

- 1 medium banana, peeled and mashed
- ¼ cup vanilla protein powder
- 1 cup rolled oats
- 1 cup almond butter
- ¼ cup unsweetened dried cranberries
- ½ tsp. ground cinnamon

1. Preheat oven to 350°F and line a baking sheet with parchment paper.
2. In a medium bowl, mix banana and protein powder. Stir in oats, almond butter, dried cranberries, and cinnamon.
3. Roll batter into eight balls and place them on the prepared baking sheet. Flatten balls slightly.
4. Bake for 20 minutes or until lightly browned.
5. Remove from oven, allow to cool slightly, and serve.

Per Serving

Calories: **301** | Fat: **17g** | Carbs: **22g** | Protein: **15g**

STUFFED AVOCADO

Prep time: **10 minutes** | Cook time: **none** | Serves **2**

- 1 (15-ounce) can black beans, drained and rinsed
- 1 (15-ounce) can sweet corn, drained
- 1 Roma tomato, diced
- 2 tbsp. chopped cilantro
- Juice of 1 lime
- 1 garlic clove, minced
- Pinch salt
- Freshly ground black pepper
- 1 small avocado, halved and pitted

1. In a small bowl, mix the black beans, corn, tomato, and cilantro. Add the lime juice and garlic, then season with salt and pepper.
2. Divide the bean salad between the avocado halves and serve.

Per Serving

Calories: **449** | Fat: **14g** | Protein: **18g** | Carbs: **71g**

COTTAGE CHEESECAKE

Prep time: **10 minutes** | Cook time: **25 minutes** | Serves **4**

- 4 oz of fat free cottage cheese
- 1 scoop of vanilla protein powder
- 1 packet of stevia
- 1 tbsp sugar free instant pudding mix
- 5 tbsp of low fat milk
- handful of strawberries

1. Add all the ingredients to a blender and blend until smooth.
2. Place in a bowl and top with the strawberries.
3. Place in the fridge for 20 minutes.
4. Serve and enjoy!

Per Serving

Calories: **487** | Protein: **43g** | Carbs: **53g** | Fat: **7g**

PROTEIN SNACK BOX

Prep time: 5 minutes | Cook time: 10 minutes | Serves 1

- 3 ounces sliced deli turkey breast
- ½ large green bell pepper, seeded and sliced
- ½ cup cherry tomatoes
- 1 ounce cubed or sliced cheddar cheese
- 1 large hard-cooked egg

1. Pile turkey slices in a stack and roll up to form a cylinder. Cut the cylinder crosswise into four pieces. Place turkey rolls in a glass storage container.
2. Arrange bell pepper slices, cherry tomatoes, cheese, and egg in the container. Cover and refrigerate for up to 3 days.

Per Serving

Calories: **289** | Fat: **15g** | Carbs: **9g** | Protein: **30g**

FLOURLESS CHOCOLATE CAKE

Prep time: 15 minutes | Cook time: 30 minutes | Serves 4

- ⅓ cup unsalted butter, plus more for greasing
- 4 ounces 80% dark chocolate, finely chopped
- ½ cup Truvia
- ½ cup unsweetened cocoa powder
- 3 large eggs, beaten
- 1 tsp. vanilla extract

1. Preheat the oven to 300 °F. Grease an 8-inch round cake pan with butter.
2. In a heatproof medium bowl, add chocolate and butter. Gently warm in the microwave until melted. Stir in Truvia, cocoa powder, eggs, and vanilla. Pour into prepared pan.
3. Bake for 30 minutes. Remove from the oven and let cool for 10 minutes.
4. Remove cake from the pan onto a wire rack and let cool completely. Serve and enjoy.

Per Serving

Calorie: **377** | Protein: **9 g** | Carbs: **14 g** | Fat: **34 g**

POWER PROTEIN WAFFLES

Prep time: 10 minutes | Cook time: 25 minutes | Serves 4

- 4 eggs whites
- 1 scoop of vanilla protein powder
- ½ cup of rolled oats
- 1 tsp of baking powder
- ½ tsp of stevia

1. Add all the ingredients into a blender and blend.
2. Add the mixture to a waffle iron and bake.

Per Serving

Calories: 314 | Protein: 37g | Carbs: 28g | Fat: 5g

HONEY BREAD PUDDING

Prep time: 5 minutes | Cook time: 30 minutes | Serves 4

- 4 slices whole-grain bread
- 1 cup nonfat vanilla greek yogurt
- 1 cup unsweetened almond milk
- 3 tsp. honey, divided
- 3 tbsp. vanilla protein powder
- 1 tsp. ground cinnamon

1. Cut bread into 32 small squares and place in a Mason jar or container with a lid.
2. In a small bowl, combine yogurt, almond milk, 1 tsp honey, protein powder, and cinnamon.
3. Pour yogurt mixture over bread, allowing it to fully soak in. Cover and refrigerate overnight.
4. In the morning, drizzle remaining honey on top and serve.

Per Serving

Calories: 273 | Fat: 4g | Carbs: 32g | Protein: 28g

TUNA SALAD RICE CAKES

Prep time: 5 minutes | **Cook time: 15 minutes** | Serves **3**

- 1 (6-ounce) can flaked tuna, packed in water, drained
- 1 avocado, finely chopped
- ¼ red bell pepper, chopped
- 1 celery stalk, chopped
- ¼ red onion, chopped
- 1 lemon wedge
- sea salt
- freshly ground black pepper
- 4 rice cakes or 4 large romaine lettuce leaves

1. In a medium bowl, mix the tuna, avocado, bell pepper, celery, and onion. Season with a squeeze of lemon juice, salt, and pepper.
2. Divide the tuna salad evenly between 2 airtight storage containers and seal. To serve, spread on the rice cakes or serve wrapped in 2 lettuce leaves. (If taking this meal on the go, store the rice cakes or lettuce leaves separately in a resealable plastic bag.)

Per Serving

Calories: 332 | **Fat: 16g** | **Protein: 28g** | **Carbs: 25g**

APPLE-CINNAMON FLAPJACKS

Prep time: 5 minutes | **Cook time: 40 minutes** | Makes **10 flapjacks**

- 2 scoops vanilla vegan protein powder
- 1½ cups egg whites
- 1 apple, peeled and chopped
- 2 cups rolled oats
- ¼ cup ground flaxseed
- 1 tbsp. ground cinnamon
- 2 tbsp. pure maple syrup
- 2 tsp. vanilla extract
- ⅓ cup raisins

1. In a high-powered blender, combine the protein powder, egg whites, apple, oats, flaxseed, cinnamon, maple syrup, and vanilla, and blend until smooth.
2. Heat a large nonstick skillet over medium heat. Add about ¼ cup of batter to the pan, then drop 7 to 8 raisins onto the pancake.
3. Cook until bubbles start to form on the surface and the edges start to look dry, about 3 minutes, then flip over and cook for another minute or so, or until both sides are golden brown.
4. Remove from the heat and let cool on a wire rack so the flapjack doesn't get soggy.
5. Repeat with the remaining batter.
6. Into each of 5 airtight containers, place 2 flapjacks and seal.

Per Serving

Calories: 299 | **Fat: 6g** | **Protein: 20g** | **Carbs: 47g**

CHEESECAKE IN A CUP

Prep time: **10 minutes** | Cook time: **15 minutes** | Serves **4**

For the Crust:

- ⅔ cup graham cracker crumbs
- 2 tbsp. coconut oil

For the Cheesecake Filling:

- 1 cup nonfat vanilla greek yogurt
- 1 cup low-fat cream cheese
- 1 tbsp. honey
- 2 tsp. freshly squeezed lemon juice
- 1 cup fresh blueberries, divided
- 2 tbsp. crushed pecans, divided

To Make the Crust:

1. In a small bowl, stir together the graham cracker crumbs and coconut oil. Into each of 4 round, airtight storage containers, place about 2½ tbsp. of the graham cracker crumbs and pack down using a spoon. Place in the freezer to firm up while you make the filling.

To Make the Cheesecake Filling:

2. In the bowl of a stand mixer or in a medium bowl using a hand mixer, mix the yogurt, cream cheese, honey, and lemon juice until smooth and creamy.
3. Remove the crust containers from the freezer, and to each, add about ¼ cup of the cream cheese filling. Smooth with a spoon, then top each with ¼ cup of fresh blueberries and ½ tbsp. of crushed pecans and seal.

Per Serving

Calories: **257** | Fat: **10g** | Protein: **14g** | Carbs: **30g**

BLACK BEAN BROWNIE CUPS

Prep time: **10 minutes** | Cook time: **25 minutes** | Serves **8**

- Nonstick cooking spray
- 1 (15-ounce) can black beans, drained and rinsed
- ½ cup rolled oats
- ⅓ cup maple syrup
- ¼ cup olive oil
- ¼ cup creamy 100% all-natural peanut butter
- 2 tbsp. unsweetened cocoa powder
- ½ tbsp. vanilla extract
- ½ tsp. baking powder
- ½ cup dark chocolate chips
- ¼ cup chopped walnuts

1. Preheat the oven to 350°F. Lightly spray a 12-cup muffin tin with nonstick cooking spray. Set aside.
2. In a food processor, combine the black beans, oats, maple syrup, olive oil, peanut butter, cocoa powder, vanilla, and baking powder and pulse until well combined.
3. Add the chocolate chips and pulse until combined. Transfer the brownie batter to a large bowl and fold in the walnuts. Divide the batter equally between the muffin cups.
4. Bake for 20 to 25 minutes, or until cooked. Let cool for 10 minutes before serving.
5. Refrigerate the brownies in an airtight container for up to 4 days.

Per Serving:

Calories: **303** | Fat: **18g** | Carbs: **29g** | Protein: **8g**

CHAPTER 10: HOMEMADE PROTEIN DRINKS

STRAWBERRY FIELDS SMOOTHIE

Prep time: **5 minutes** | Cook time: **15 minutes** | Serves **5**

For The Smoothie Packs:

- 5 cups frozen sliced strawberries, divided
- 5 tbsp. almond butter, divided
- 5 scoops vanilla whey or vegan protein powder, divided

For The Smoothies:

- 5 cups unsweetened vanilla almond milk, divided

To Make The Smoothie Packs:

1. In each of 5 resealable freezer bags, place 1 cup of strawberries, 1 tbsp. of almond butter, and 1 scoop of vanilla whey. Flatten, pressing any air out of the bag, and seal. Store in the freezer until ready to use.

To Make A Smoothie:

1. In a blender, combine 1 cup of almond milk and the contents of 1 smoothie pack. Blend until smooth.

Per Serving

Calories: **258** | Fat: **13g** | Protein: **25g** | Carbs: **13g**

PEANUT BUTTER AND BANANA SMOOTHIE

Prep time: **5 minutes** | Cook time: **10 minutes** | Serves **1**

- 1 medium banana, peeled and frozen
- 2 tbsp. smooth peanut butter
- 1 ¼ cups vanilla almond milk
- ¼ cup vanilla protein powder
- ½ tsp. vanilla extract
- ¼ tsp. ground cinnamon

1. Combine all ingredients in a blender and process until smooth. Pour into a tall glass and serve immediately.

Per Serving

Calories: **451** | Fat: **19g** | Carbs: **38g** | Protein: **34g**

SUNNY CITRUS SMOOTHIE

Prep time: **5 minutes** | Cook time: **10 minutes** | Serves **5**

For The Smoothie Packs:

- 1¼ cups frozen pineapple chunks, divided
- 1¼ cups frozen papaya chunks, divided
- 1¼ cups frozen mango chunks, divided
- 2½ fresh or frozen bananas, chopped, divided
- 2½ tbsp. ground flaxseed, divided

For The Smoothies:

- 2½ cups nonfat vanilla greek yogurt, divided
- 2½ cups orange juice, divided

To Make The Smoothie Packs:

1. Into each of 5 resealable freezer bags, place ¼ cup of pineapple, ¼ cup of papaya, ¼ cup of mango, half a banana, and ½ tbsp. of flaxseed. Flatten, pressing any air out of the bag, and seal. Store in the freezer until ready to use.

To Make A Smoothie:

1. In a blender, combine ½ cup of yogurt, ½ cup of orange juice, and the contents of 1 smoothie pack, and blend until smooth.

Per Serving

Calories: **273** | Fat: **2g** | Protein: **13g** | Carbs: **63g**

GO GREEN SMOOTHIE

Prep time: **5 minutes** | Cook time: **5 minutes** | Serves **2**

- 3 cups fresh baby spinach
- 1 large banana
- 1 cup skim milk
- 1 cup nonfat plain Greek yogurt
- ½ cup fresh blueberries
- ½ cup rolled oats
- ⅛ cup 100% all-natural almond butter
- 1 tbsp. hemp hearts

1. Combine the spinach, banana, milk, yogurt, blueberries, oats, almond butter, and hemp hearts in a blender and puree until smooth.
2. Pour into 2 glasses and serve.

Per Serving

Calories: **383** | Fat: **11g** | Carbs: **49g** | Protein: **26g**

PUMPKIN POWER

Prep time: **10 minutes** | Cook time: **25 minutes** | Serves **4**

- 2 scoops of vanilla protein powder
- 1 cup of chopped pumpkin
- 1 tsp cinnamon
- 1 cup of water

1. Add all the ingredients to a blender and blend until smooth.
2. Enjoy.

Per Serving

Calories: **224** | Protein: **38g** | Carbs: **14g** | Fat: **3g**

AVOCADO-MINT PROTEIN SMOOTHIE

Prep time: **5 minutes** | Cook time: **none** | Serves **1**

- 1 cup unsweetened almond milk
- 4 fresh mint leaves
- 1 banana, peeled and sliced
- ½ medium avocado, peeled and pitted
- 3 whole dates (2.5 ounces), pitted
- 1 tbsp. dark chocolate chips
- 1 scoop vanilla protein powder

1. Into a blender, add almond milk, mint, banana, avocado, dates, chocolate chips, and protein powder.
2. Blend ingredients until smooth. Pour smoothie into a glass and serve.

Per Serving

Calorie: **664** | Protein: **29 g** | Carbs: **103 g** | Fat: **22 g**

NEAPOLITAN SMOOTHIE

Prep time: **5 minutes** | Cook time: **5 minutes** | Serves **1**

- 1 scoop vanilla protein powder
- 4 frozen strawberries
- 1 tsp. cocoa powder
- 1 tsp. sugar-free Hershey's chocolate syrup
- 1 packet stevia
- 3–4 ice cubes

1. In a blender, blend all ingredients until smooth. Serve immediately.

Per Serving

Calories: **141** | Fat: **1 g** | Protein: **21 g** | Carbs: **15 g**

BERRYLICIOUS PROTEIN SMOOTHIE

Prep time: **5 minutes** | Cook time: **20 minutes** | Serves **5**

- 5 cups frozen mixed berries, divided
- 2½ fresh or frozen bananas, divided
- 2½ cups chopped kale, divided
- 5 scoops vanilla vegan protein powder, divided
- 5 tbsp. ground flaxseed, divided
- 5 tbsp. chia seeds, divided
- 5 cups unsweetened vanilla almond milk, divided

1. Into each of 5 resealable freezer bags, put 1 cup of berries, half a banana, ½ cup of kale, 1 scoop of protein powder, 1 tbsp. of flaxseed, and 1 tbsp. of chia seeds. Lay the bags flat, and remove as much air as possible before sealing.
2. To use a smoothie pack, pour 1 cup of almond milk into a blender, followed by the contents of 1 smoothie pack, and blend until smooth.

Per Serving

Calories: **413** | Fat: **13g** | Protein: **32g** | Carbs: **50g**

STRAWBERRY CHEESECAKE SMOOTHIE

Prep time: **5 minutes** | Cook time: **2 minutes** | Serves **2**

- 2 cups frozen strawberries
- 2½ cups reduced-fat milk
- 1½ cups nonfat or low-fat plain Greek yogurt
- 2 scoops whey protein powder
- 4 tbsp. low-fat cream cheese

1. In a blender, combine the strawberries, milk, yogurt, whey, and cream cheese.
2. Process on high for 1 to 2 minutes, until smooth. Add more liquid or ice as needed for the desired consistency.

Per Serving

Calories: **537** | Fat: **13g** | Protein: **58g** | Carbs: **48g**

CHOCO COFFEE ENERGY SHAKE

Prep time: **10 minutes** | Cook time: **25 minutes** | Serves **4**

- 2 scoops of chocolate protein powder
- I cup of low-fat milk
- 1 cup of water
- 1 tbsp of instant coffee

1. Add all the ingredients to a blender and blend until smooth.
2. Enjoy.

Per Serving

Calories: **299** | Protein: **42g** | Carbs: **14g** | Fat: **6g**

MEASUREMENT CONVERSION CHART

VOLUME EQUIVALENTS(DRY)

US STANDARD	METRIC (APPROXIMATE)
1/8 teaspoon	0.5 mL
1/4 teaspoon	1 mL
1/2 teaspoon	2 mL
3/4 teaspoon	4 mL
1 teaspoon	5 mL
1 tablespoon	15 mL
1/4 cup	59 mL
1/2 cup	118 mL
3/4 cup	177 mL
1 cup	235 mL
2 cups	475 mL
3 cups	700 mL
4 cups	1 L

VOLUME EQUIVALENTS(LIQUID)

US STANDARD	US STANDARD (OUNCES)	METRIC (APPROXIMATE)
2 tablespoons	1 fl.oz.	30 mL
1/4 cup	2 fl.oz.	60 mL
1/2 cup	4 fl.oz.	120 mL
1 cup	8 fl.oz.	240 mL
1 1/2 cup	12 fl.oz.	355 mL
2 cups or 1 pint	16 fl.oz.	475 mL
4 cups or 1 quart	32 fl.oz.	1 L
1 gallon	128 fl.oz.	4 L

TEMPERATURES EQUIVALENTS

FAHRENHEIT(F)	CELSIUS(C) (APPROXIMATE)
225 °F	107 °C
250 °F	120 °C
275 °F	135 °C
300 °F	150 °C
325 °F	160 °C
350 °F	180 °C
375 °F	190 °C
400 °F	205 °C
425 °F	220 °C
450 °F	235 °C
475 °F	245 °C
500 °F	260 °C

WEIGHT EQUIVALENTS

US STANDARD	METRIC (APPROXIMATE)
1 ounce	28 g
2 ounces	57 g
5 ounces	142 g
10 ounces	284 g
15 ounces	425 g
16 ounces (1 pound)	455 g
1.5 pounds	680 g
2 pounds	907 g

The Dirty Dozen and Clean Fifteen

The Environmental Working Group (EWG) is a nonprofit, nonpartisan organization dedicated to protecting human health and the environment Its mission is to empower people to live healthier lives in a healthier environment. This organization publishes an annual list of the twelve kinds of produce, in sequence, that have the highest amount of pesticide residue-the Dirty Dozen-as well as a list of the fifteen kinds ofproduce that have the least amount of pesticide residue-the Clean Fifteen.

THE DIRTY DOZEN	THE CLEAN FIFTEEN
• The 2016 Dirty Dozen includes the following produce. These are considered among the year's most important produce to buy organic:	• The least critical to buy organically are the Clean Fifteen list. The following are on the 2016 list:

THE DIRTY DOZEN

Strawberries	Spinach
Apples	Tomatoes
Nectarines	Bell peppers
Peaches	Cherry tomatoes
Celery	Cucumbers
Grapes	Kale/collard greens
Cherries	Hot peppers

• *The Dirty Dozen list contains two additional itemskale/collard greens and hot peppers-because they tend to contain trace levels of highly hazardous pesticides.*

THE CLEAN FIFTEEN

Avocados	Papayas
Corn	Kiw
Pineapples	Eggplant
Cabbage	Honeydew
Sweet peas	Grapefruit
Onions	Cantaloupe
Asparagus	Cauliflower
Mangos	

• *Some of the sweet corn sold in the United States are made from genetically engineered (GE) seedstock. Buy organic varieties of these crops to avoid GE produce.*

APPENDIX 3: INDEX

Hey there!

Wow, can you believe we've reached the end of this culinary journey together? I'm truly thrilled and filled with joy as I think back on all the recipes we've shared and the flavors we've discovered. This experience, blending a bit of tradition with our own unique twists, has been a journey of love for good food. And knowing you've been out there, giving these dishes a try, has made this adventure incredibly special to me.

Even though we're turning the last page of this book, I hope our conversation about all things delicious doesn't have to end. I cherish your thoughts, your experiments, and yes, even those moments when things didn't go as planned. Every piece of feedback you share is invaluable, helping to enrich this experience for us all.

I'd be so grateful if you could take a moment to share your thoughts with me, be it through a review on Amazon or any other place you feel comfortable expressing yourself online. Whether it's praise, constructive criticism, or even an idea for how we might do things differently in the future, your input is what truly makes this journey meaningful.

This book is a piece of my heart, offered to you with all the love and enthusiasm I have for cooking. But it's your engagement and your words that elevate it to something truly extraordinary.

Thank you from the bottom of my heart for being such an integral part of this culinary adventure. Your openness to trying new things and sharing your experiences has been the greatest gift.

Catch you later,

Renee R. Legere

Made in the USA
Las Vegas, NV
04 January 2025